Copyright © 2024 BY April W. Mullican

TABLE OF CONTENT

Map Of New Zealand

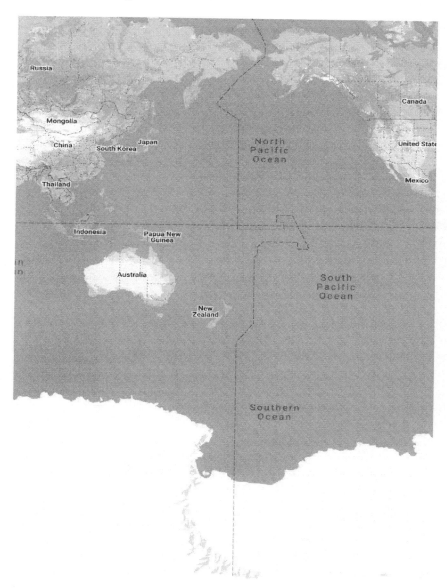

INTRODUCTION

Welcome to New Zealand, a land of wild wonders and limitless adventure. Situated in the southwestern Pacific Ocean, this island nation offers a kaleidoscope of unusual activities and stunning landscapes that entice travellers.

Peruse the pages of this travel guide and picture the untamed grandeur of snow-capped mountains, the tranquillity of clear lakes, and the cultural mosaic created by the welcoming Kiwi people.

Each city has its narrative to tell, from Auckland's cosmopolitan charm to Queenstown's enchanting landscapes. Get a handle on the planning process by reading up on cultural differences, travel logistics, and finances— Marvel at the landscape's thriving museums, bustling marketplaces, and historic monuments. Savour the region's flavours as you raise a glass to its specialities. Put your health and safety first by following practical safety tips.

Standing on the brink of this island kingdom, a world of unparalleled beauty unfolds before you.

Encased in snow, the Southern Alps are guardians of time's mysteries.

Consider Lake Wakatipu's shimmering waters, a liquid mirror reflecting the magnificence of the surrounding highlands. New Zealand is a dynamic tapestry of awe-inspiring marvels, from the geothermal splendour of Rotorua to the ancient glowworm-lit caverns of Waitomo.

This excursion, however, is more than just a tour of natural wonders; it is an immersion into the pulsating heart of a culture as vibrant as the colours of a Pacific sunset.

The stories of Maori warriors resonate through the valleys, while the modern rhythm of towns merges with the ancient narratives delivered by the wind.

What makes New Zealand so unique? Because it's more than merely a location; it's a symphony of experiences waiting for you to design. You are not just a visitor as you navigate this guide; you are the storyteller of your adventure.

Join us on a trip where planning becomes a canvas for your goals, and each decision is a brushstroke in constructing your own New Zealand masterpiece.

Allow this book to be your muse and compass, from the practicalities of budgeting to the rhythmic beat of Maori haka.

As you turn the pages, imagine your ideal experience and dream getaway unfolding across New Zealand's cities.

Allow this guide to be your companion as you blaze the trail to an exceptional journey that surpasses the ordinary and generates memories to last a lifetime.

Join us on this journey through the heart of Aotearoa, where every chapter is a fresh discovery, and every moment is an opportunity to tell your tale.

Welcome to New Zealand, where dreams come true, and the journey is just as incredible as the destination.

Chapter 1: Discovering New Zealand

HISTORY

The primary settlement period of New Zealand (Aotearoa) began between 1320 and 1350 CE when it was discovered and settled by Polynesians, who built a separate Mori culture.

Abel Tasman, a Dutch sailor, was the first European explorer known to have visited New Zealand on December 13, 1642. The Treaty of Waitangi was signed in 1840 by representatives of the United Kingdom and various Mori chiefs, bringing New Zealand into the British Empire and granting Mori the same rights as British people.

Disputes over conflicting interpretations of the Treaty and colonial ambition to purchase territory from Mori sparked the New Zealand Wars in 1843. Since the late 18th century, explorers and other mariners, missionaries, traders, and adventurers have routinely visited the country.

In the 1850s, the colony gained responsible government. Beginning in the 1890s, the New Zealand Parliament enacted progressive legislation, such as women's suffrage and old-age pensions.

After becoming a self-governing Dominion of the British Empire in 1907, New Zealand remained an enthusiastic empire member, with over 100,000 New Zealanders serving in the New Zealand Expeditionary Force during World War I.

GEOGRAPHY

New Zealand is an island nation in the southwestern Pacific Ocean, close to the centre of the aquatic hemisphere. It comprises hundreds of islands, most remnants of an enormous continent now submerged beneath the water.

The South Island (or Te Waipounamu) and the North Island (or Te Ika-a-Mui) are separated by the Cook Strait. Stewart

Island / Rakiura, located 30 kilometres (19 miles) off the coast of the South Island across Foveaux Strait, is the third-largest. Other islands are much smaller in size.

The three largest islands span 1,600 kilometres (990 miles) and are between 35° and 47° south latitudes.

New Zealand is the world's sixth-largest island country, with a land area of 268,710 km2 (103,750 sq mi). The landscapes of the country range from the fjords of the southwest to the sandy beaches of the subtropical Far North.

The Southern Alps dominate the South Island, while a volcanic plateau dominates much of the central North Island.

The terrain is rugged primarily or hilly, with volcanic peaks in the heart of the North Island and fiords in the extreme southwest.

The country is located on the tectonic plates of the Pacific and Australian plates, making it one of the world's most active earthquake and volcanic regions. Several devastating earthquakes throughout its history have hit the country,

New Zealand's climate is temperate, with some tundra and subantarctic areas. Temperatures frequently drop below 0 °C

(32 °F) and rise over 30 °C (86 °F). Conditions range from rainy and cold on the west coast of the South Island to dry and continental, a short distance distant across the highlands and to a tundra-like environment in Southland's Deep South. The country has no land borders and a coastline of 15,134 km (9,404 mi). The highest point in New Zealand is Aoraki / Mount Cook, which is 3,724 meters (12,218 feet) above sea level, and the lowest point is Taieri Plain, which is -2 meters. The Waikato River is New Zealand's longest river, stretching 425 kilometres (264 miles), while Lake Taupo is the largest lake, with an area of 3,487 kilometres (1,346 square miles). New Zealand's natural resources include natural gas, iron ore, sand, coal, timber, hydropower, gold, and limestone. The country also has a diverse flora and fauna, including several endemic species such as the kiwi bird, tuatara, and kauri tree.

CULTURE

New Zealand has a rich and diversified culture that its distinct history and geography have shaped. New Zealand's culture is a mash-up of indigenous Mori, colonial British, and other cultural influences.

The country's first inhabitants brought Polynesian customs and language, and amid centuries of seclusion, they developed their own Mori and Moriori civilizations. In the nineteenth century, British immigrants brought Western culture and significantly impacted the indigenous residents, spreading Western religious traditions and the English language.

Over time, a distinct Pkeh or New Zealand European culture developed. Recent immigration from the Pacific, East Asia, and South Asia has increased New Zealand's cultural variety.

New Zealand's significant cultural influence remains Western, heavily emphasizing democracy and egalitarianism.

Mori culture is an integral part of the national identity, and ongoing efforts to maintain and honour the Mori language and traditions are being made.

Mori people have a rich cultural history deeply rooted in the land and water. They have a rich storytelling tradition passed down through generations through songs, chants, and legends.

Mori art is also an essential part of their culture, with intricate carvings and weavings used to tell stories and express meaning. Kapa haka is a traditional Mori performing art that is also essential to Mori culture. It is often performed at cultural gatherings and festivals and comprises singing, dancing, and chanting.

New Zealand is also known for its distinctive cuisine, which combines Mori, European, and Pacific Island influences. Popular dishes include fish and chips, meat pies, pavlova, and hokey pokey ice cream.

The country is also well-known for its wine, with regions such as Marlborough and Hawke's Bay producing some of the world's best Sauvignon Blanc and Pinot Noir.

Sports are essential to New Zealand culture, with rugby union being the most popular sport.

The All Blacks, New Zealand's national rugby team, are one of the most successful teams in the world, with a massive following both in New Zealand and worldwide. Cricket, netball, and football are also popular sports.

New Zealand also has a robust arts and creative sector, contributing significantly to the economy. According to the Ministry of Culture and Heritage, the arts and creative sector contributed $14.9 billion to New Zealand's GDP for the fiscal year ending March 2022, accounting for 4.2% of the entire economy and the highest contribution since records began in 2000.

As of March 2022, 115,000 people were primarily employed in the creative sector (32% were self-employed).

Chapter 2: Planning Your Trip

BUDGETING (HOW TO SAVE MONEY)

If you're considering vacationing in New Zealand, money is integral to planning. According to Budget Your Trip, you should budget $140 (NZ$229) daily for your New Zealand vacation.

This is the average daily price based on other tourists' expenditures. Previous visitors spent an average of $32 (NZ$52) on meals, $21 (NZ$34) on local transportation, and $144 (NZ$235) on accommodation in a single day.

On average, a one-week trip to New Zealand for two people costs about $1,967 (NZ$3,209). Hotel, food, local transportation, and sightseeing are all included. A two-week trip to New Zealand costs about $3,933 (NZ$6,418) for two people.

Lodging, food, local transportation, and sightseeing are all included in this price. Please remember that pricing can vary depending on your travel style, pace, and other factors. 1. If you want to save money on your trip to New Zealand, consider the following suggestions:

Visiting during The Off-Season: The peak tourism season in New Zealand is from December to February.

You can save money on flights, accommodation, and activities if you visit during the off-season.

Stay In Hostels Or Low-Cost Hotels: Accommodation in New Zealand can be expensive, but staying in hostels or low-cost hotels can help you save money.

Cook Your Meals: Eating out in New Zealand may be expensive. To save money, consider preparing your meals if you can access a kitchen.

Use Public Transportation: Renting a car in New Zealand may be costly. If you're on a tight budget, consider taking public transit.

Take Advantage Of Free Activities: Hiking, visiting beaches, and exploring national parks are free in New Zealand. Utilize these to save money on your trip.

WHEN TO VISIT

New Zealand is a lovely nation that may be visited all year. However, the best time to visit New Zealand is determined by what you want to do and see during your stay. Here are some things to think about when planning your visit:

Summer (January to February): New Zealand's busiest tourism season, and with good reason. The weather is pleasant and sunny, making it an ideal time to visit the country's excellent beaches, trekking, or engage in outdoor sports such as kayaking and bungee jumping.

The days are long, with daylight lasting until around 9 pm, providing ample opportunity for exploration. However, because this is the busiest time of year, expect crowds and higher prices.

Autumn (March to May): If you want to avoid crowds and enjoy cooler weather, visit New Zealand in the autumn.

The leaves change colour, creating a beautiful backdrop for hiking and sightseeing. The weather is still great, and fewer tourists make this an excellent time to visit the country's national parks and other attractions.

Winter (June to August): If you enjoy winter sports such as skiing and snowboarding, winter is the best time to visit New Zealand. The country's ski resorts are world-class, and the scenery is stunning. The temperature is bitterly cold, but the snow-capped mountains and glaciers create a breathtaking backdrop.

Winter is also the low season so that you may get great deals on lodging and activities.

From September until November: If you want to see the country's stunning wildflowers in bloom, visit New Zealand in the spring. The weather is pleasant, and the crowds are still manageable. It's a great time to go hiking or visit one of the many vineyards in the country. However, the weather might be unpredictable, so dress accordingly.

Overall, the best time to visit New Zealand is determined by what you want to do and see there. Summer is the best time to visit to enjoy the nice weather and outdoor activities.

If you enjoy winter sports, winter is the best time to visit. However, regardless of when you visit, you will fall in love with New Zealand's magnificent beauty and kind people.

GETTING THERE

Flying is the quickest, easiest, and least expensive way to visit New Zealand. There are no international passenger ferries, so unless you own a boat, you must join a cruise, crew on a private yacht, or pay for your passage on a cargo ship (a rewarding experience for people who like sea journeys).

Airfares vary according to season, with the highest rates available during the New Zealand summer (Dec-Feb); lower rates are available during the shoulder seasons (Sept-Nov & March-May), and the lowest rates are available during the quiet (ski) season (June-Aug).

If you're flying into New Zealand from Australia, your only real options are the international airports in Auckland and Christchurch. However, there are fewer direct flights to Christchurch, and several scheduled airlines offer a free codeshare shuttle from Auckland. An open-jaw ticket (flying into one and out of the other) is frequently less expensive than a conventional return.

Tourists and people on short-term job visas are usually required by New Zealand immigration to have an outbound ticket. Therefore, one-way tickets are only viable for Australian and New Zealand citizens.

If you've purchased a return ticket and decide you want to stay longer or take a completely alternative route, you can change the dates and, in rare cases, the way with the airline or travel agent, depending on the limits of your ticket, but there may be a cost.

Auckland Airport (AKL) is a central airline hub and the busiest airport for international flights.

TRAVELLING DOCUMENT

PASSPORTS AND VISAS FOR ENTRY INTO NEW ZEALAND

- If you are not a New Zealand or Australian citizen, you may need to apply for a visa or a New Zealand Electronic Travel Authority (NZeTA) to travel to or transit through New Zealand.
- Remember to check travel restrictions for any countries/regions you'll pass through in transit and on your return trip.
- All passengers entering New Zealand can complete a New Zealand Traveller Declaration instead of a paper Passenger Arrival Card. Passengers transiting abroad are exempt from filing a declaration.

NEW ZEALAND TRANSPORTATION

Suppose you are not a New Zealand or Australian citizen. In that case, you may be required to obtain a visa or a New Zealand Electronic Travel Authority (NZeTA) to transit through New Zealand.

Remember to check the entry criteria for your final destination.

COVID-19

Visitors do not need to show proof of vaccination or take a pre-departure test to enter New Zealand.

Passengers are not required to show proof of vaccination or take a pre-departure test when flying with Air New Zealand. We ask that you reconsider your travel plans if you feel ill and test positive for COVID-19.

THE WEATHER AND THE CLIMATE

The climate of New Zealand varies greatly, with the north of the North Island experiencing balmy subtropical weather in summer and the alpine regions of the South Island seeing heavy snow and temperatures as low as -10 °C (14°F) in winter.

The country's climate is influenced by its Southern Hemisphere location, the prevailing westerly winds, and the ocean currents surrounding it.

According to a Ministry of Environment assessment, New Zealand's climate is warming, with annual average temperatures rising at 28 of 30 sites around the country and all 30 during winter.

Eighteen of the thirty locations had a very likely increasing trend in the number of heat wave days, while 12 had a very likely decreasing trend in the number of frost days. Civil society and the New Zealand government respond to climate change in various ways.

This includes participating in international treaties and social and political conversations about climate change. New Zealand has an emissions trading scheme, and the government introduced the Climate Change Response (Zero Carbon) Amendment Bill in 2019, establishing a Climate Change Commission to advise the government on policies and emissions budgets.

In 2019, New Zealand made various climate change mitigation goals, including reducing net carbon emissions to zero by 2050, planting 1 billion trees by 2028, and incorporating pastoral agriculture (farmers) into an emissions price scheme by 2025.

LOCAL CUSTOM AND ETIQUETTE

New Zealand has a rich and diversified culture that its distinct history and geography have shaped. New Zealand's culture is a mash-up of indigenous Mori, colonial British, and other cultural influences.

The country's first inhabitants brought Polynesian customs and language, and amid centuries of seclusion, they developed their own Mori and Moriori civilizations. In the nineteenth century, British immigrants brought Western culture and significantly impacted the indigenous residents, spreading Western religious traditions and the English language.

Over time, a distinct Pkeh or New Zealand European culture developed. Recent immigration from the Pacific, East Asia, and South Asia has increased New Zealand's cultural variety.

New Zealand's significant cultural influence remains Western, heavily emphasizing democracy and egalitarianism. Mori culture is an integral part of the national identity, and ongoing efforts are being made to maintain and honour the Mori language and traditions.

Mori people have a rich cultural history deeply rooted in the land and water. They have a rich storytelling tradition that is passed down through generations in the form of songs, chants, and legends. Mori art is also an essential part of their culture, with intricate carvings and weavings used to tell stories and express meaning.

Kapa haka is a traditional Mori performing art that is also essential to Mori culture.

It is often performed at cultural gatherings and festivals and comprises singing, dancing, and chanting.

There are a few things to keep in mind when it comes to New Zealand etiquette. New Zealanders are generally friendly and welcoming to visitors, but respecting local customs and traditions is critical. Here are some pointers:

People should be greeted as follows: New Zealanders are generally informal and address one other using first names. A handshake is a standard greeting, although other individuals prefer hongi, a traditional Mori greeting that involves rubbing noses together.

Taking off Your Shoes: It is customary in New Zealand to remove them before entering someone's home. This is especially true if you are visiting a Mori marae, a site of communal gathering for Mori people.

Tipping is not customary in New Zealand, but it is appreciated if you receive excellent service.

Formal attire is required. New Zealanders are generally casual dressers, yet it is critical to dress appropriately for the occasion. You should wear a suit or a dress if you're going to a formal event.

Food and Drink: New Zealanders are known for their love of food and beverages. If you are invited to someone's home for a meal, it is customary to bring a small gift, such as a bottle of wine or a box of chocolates. It's also important to try local dishes like fish and chips, meat pies, and pavlova.

LANGUAGE SPOKEN

English, Mori, and New Zealand Sign Language are the three official languages of New Zealand. English is the most widely spoken language in New Zealand, with 95.4% of the population saying it is the first language or competent as a second.

Regarding pronunciation, New Zealand English is most similar to Australian English, with a few key differences. Mori is New Zealand's second most spoken language, with about 4% of the people speaking it.

In 1987, the Mori language of the indigenous Mori people was declared the first de jure official language. Since 2006, New Zealand Sign Language (NZSL) has been an official language. Minority ethnic populations in New Zealand speak a variety of extra languages.

USEFUL TRAVEL PHRASES

Here are some common travel phrases that can help you communicate with locals and make your trip more enjoyable:

- Kia ora - A simple greeting that can be used at any time of day. It is a Māori phrase that means "be well" or "be healthy".
- Haere mai - A way to say "welcome" in Māori. It is often used when greeting visitors to New Zealand.
- Kei te pehea koe? - A way to ask "how are you?" in Māori. It is pronounced "kay-teh-peh-ha-koy".
- Ka kite anō - A way to say "see you later" in Māori. It is pronounced "kah-kee-teh-ah-noh".
- Sweet as - A common Kiwi phrase that means "all good" or "no problem". It is often used in response to a request or question.
- Jandals is a Kiwi term for flip-flops or sandals.
- The chilly bin is a Kiwi term for a cooler or icebox.
- Togs - This is a Kiwi term for swimwear.
- BYO - This Kiwi term stands for "bring your own". It is often used when referring to a party or event

where guests are expected to bring their food or drinks.

- Fush and Chups - this is a Kiwi term for fish and chips.
- Whakapai hauora: Good health (used instead of 'bless you' after a sneeze).
- Whakapau kaha: Excuse me.
- Kei hea te wharepaku? Where is the bathroom?
- Haere ki te whare whakararuraru: Go to the information center.

Chapter 3: Getting Around the Major Cities

AUCKLAND

Auckland is the largest city in New Zealand, located in the North Island. It has an urban population of roughly 1,478,800 (June 2023) and is the most populated city in New Zealand and the fifth largest city in Oceania.

Auckland is a big metropolitan city with a diversified culture that its unique history and geography have moulded.

The human history of the Auckland metropolitan area stretches from early Māori settlers in the 14th century to the first European explorers in the late 18th century, over a short stretch as the official capital of (European-settled) New Zealand in the middle of the 19th century to its current position as the fastest-growing and commercially dominating metropolis of the country.

The Māori people have a rich cultural past strongly connected with the land and sea. Māori culture continues to be an integral aspect of the national identity, with continual attempts to respect and honour the Māori language and Māori traditions.

Auckland is also noted for its unusual cuisine, blending Māori, European, and Pacific Island influences. Some of the most popular delicacies include fish and chips, meat pies, pavlova, and hokey pokey ice cream.

Auckland is a city of many attractions. The Sky Tower is one of the most famous monuments in Auckland, giving panoramic views of the city from its observation deck. The Auckland Harbour Bridge is another famous attraction, offering a unique bungy jumping experience.

The Auckland War Memorial Museum is a terrific site to learn about the history of New Zealand, and the Auckland Domain is a gorgeous park suitable for a picnic or a stroll.

ATTRACTION SITES
THE AUCKLAND WAR MEMORIAL MUSEUM

The Auckland War Memorial Museum Tāmaki Paenga Hira is one of New Zealand's most important museums and war memorials. It is located in the Auckland Domain, a huge park in central Auckland. The museum's neoclassical edifice was created in the 1920s and 1950s and stands on Observatory Hill, the remains of a dormant volcano.

The museum's collections and exhibits began in 1852 and have grown to encompass over 4.5 million pieces.

The Auckland War Memorial Museum is a memorial site for those who have served and suffered for New Zealand. It is also a site of learning, including displays covering New Zealand's history, natural history, and military history.

The museum's holdings are grouped into numerous sections, including Māori, Pacific, and European collections. The Māori collection comprises taonga (treasures) such as sculptures, weaponry, and textiles, while the Pacific collection includes antiquities from across the Pacific region. The European collection contains art, ornamental arts, and social history objects.

The World War I Hall of Memories is one of the most popular displays at the Auckland War Memorial Museum.

This exhibit remembers the 18,000 New Zealanders who perished in World War I and displays a reproduction of a World War I battlefield, complete with trenches and artillery. Another popular exhibit is the Māori Court, which comprises a meeting house and other Māori antiquities.

The museum is open from 10 am to 5 pm, except for Christmas Day.

Admission is free for Auckland residents with proof of address, but non-residents are charged a fee. Guided tours are offered for an extra cost.

EDEN GARDEN

Eden Garden is a magnificent garden in the middle of Auckland, New Zealand. It is situated on the slopes of Mount Eden and is set on 2 hectares of former quarry land. The garden was established in 1964 and is open to the public for an admission fee. It was donated to the people of New

Zealand in 1965 and is managed by The Eden Garden Society, Inc., a not-for-profit society.

Eden Garden is a haven of peace and beauty that offers a unique look into the flora of New Zealand.

The garden's many collections of plants include what is reputed to be the most extensive collection of camellias in New Zealand, vineyards (tropical rhododendrons), some of which are always in bloom, Japanese maples, magnolias, hibiscus, bromeliads, native trees, interesting rock formations, waterfalls, and a spectacular perennial garden. The garden is a lovely area to explore and relax, with something new to find on every visit.

In recent years, the annual spring Eden Garden Tulip Festival has been one of Auckland's biggest and most significant. The festival is held over a weekend in late August/early September and is a celebration of the garden's beautiful tulips.

There is always something of interest in bloom in Eden Garden, making it a popular destination for locals and tourists alike.

Eden Garden is open from 9 am to 4 pm, Tuesday to Sunday. As a charitable organization, the garden demands a donation for admittance, which helps with garden operations and guarantees families may continue to visit their loved ones. The park also offers guided tours for an extra cost.

WAIHEKE ISLAND

Waiheke Island is the second-largest island in the Hauraki Gulf of New Zealand, after Great Barrier Island. It is approximately 21.5 km (13.4 mi) from the central city terminal in Auckland.

The island is 19.3 km (12.0 mi) in length from west to east, ranges in width from 0.64 to 9.65 km (0.40 to 6.00 mi), and has a surface area of 92 km² (36 sq mi).

The coastline is 133.5 km (83.0 mi) and 40 km (25 mi) of beaches. The island is quite steep with few flat areas, the highest peak being Maunganui at 231 m (758 ft).

Waiheke Island is a popular location for visitors and locals alike. It is noted for its magnificent beaches, rolling hills, and wineries. The island is home to over 30 vineyards, several providing wine tastings and excursions. The island's climate is slightly milder than Auckland, with less humidity and rain and more sunny hours.

The island is also home to various art galleries, cafes, and eateries. The main town on the island is Oneroa, which contains a variety of stores, cafes, and restaurants. Other popular sites on the island include Palm Beach, Onetangi Beach, and the Stony Batter Historic Reserve.

Waiheke Island is accessible by ferry from Auckland. The ferry station is located in Matiatia Bay at the western extremity of the island. The island is also accessible via helicopter and private boat.

QUEENSTOWN

Queenstown is a resort town in the southwest of New Zealand's South Island. It has an urban population of 29,000 (June 2023) and is built around an inlet called Queenstown Bay on Lake Wakatipu, a long, thin, Z-shaped lake formed by glacial processes, and has views of nearby mountains such as The Remarkables, Cecil Peak, Walter Peak and just above the town, Ben Lomond and Queenstown Hill. The city is noted for its commerce-oriented tourism, especially adventure and ski tourism.

The area was discovered and first populated by Māori. Kāi Tahu says that the lake was dug by the Waitaha ancestor,

Rākaihautū, with his kō (digging staff) named Tūwhakaroria. After arriving at Whakatū in the waka Uruao, Rākaihautū divided his crew into two.

He led one group through the heart of Te Waipounamu, digging the island's freshwater lakes. After creating the lakes Hāwea, Wānaka, and Whakatipu Waimāori, he travelled through the Greenstone Hollyford valleys until ultimately searching Whakatipu Waitai (Lake McKerrow).

The first non-Māori to visit Lake Wakatipu was European Nathanael Chalmers, who was taken by Reko, the head of the Tuturau, over the Waimea Plains and up the Mataura River in September 1853.

European explorers William Gilbert Rees and Nicholas von Tunzelmann were the first non-Māori to colonize the area.

Rees established a high country farm at the position of Queenstown's current town core in 1860, but the finding of gold in the Arrow River in 1862 inspired Rees to turn his wool shed into a hotel named the Queen's Arms, today known as Eichardt's. Many Queenstown streets bear names from the gold mining era (such as Camp Street), and some historic buildings remain.

Queenstown is a popular destination for visitors and locals alike. It is noted for its magnificent beaches, rolling hills, and wineries. The town is also home to various art galleries, cafes, and restaurants.

The main town on the island is Oneroa, which contains a variety of stores, cafes, and restaurants. Other popular sites on the island include Palm Beach, Onetangi Beach, and the Stony Batter Historic Reserve.

ATTRACTION SITES
LAKE WAKATIPU

Lake Wakatipu is an inland lake in the South Island of New Zealand. It is located in the southwest corner of the Otago area, on its boundary with Southland.

The lake is 80 kilometres long, making it New Zealand's longest lake and, at 289 km², it's third largest. The lake is also bottomless, having a maximum depth of 420 meters.

It sits at 310 meters, towards the southern edge of the Southern Alps. The topography is an inverted "N" form or "dog leg".

The Dart River pours into the northern end; the lake then goes south for 30 kilometres before turning sharply to the east. Twenty kilometres farther along, it swings sharply to the south, reaching its southern end 30 kilometres further south, near Kingston.

The lake is drained by the Kawarau River, which runs out from the lake's single arm, the Frankton Arm, 8 km east of Queenstown.

Lake Wakatipu is recognized for its gorgeous scenery and is surrounded by mountains. Two mountain ranges, the Remarkables and the Tapuae-o-Uenuku/Hector Mountains, sit along its southeastern side. It is a familiar venue for adventure tourism, with ski fields, paragliding, bungy jumping and tramping paths within easy reach.

A vintage steamboat, the TSS Earnslaw routinely plies its waters.

SKYLINE QUEENSTOWN

Skyline Queenstown is a renowned tourist attraction service in Queenstown, New Zealand. It provides a gondola, with a café at the top station and a luge returning to the base station. The entire terminal building is situated on the slopes of the Ben Lomond mountain peak 450 metres (1,480 ft) above the level of Lake Wakatipu. It has numerous activities, such as a gondola, a luge, a mountain bike park, and hiking places.

The main complex contains amenities such as a restaurant, bar, cafe, and gift shop. The gondola lifts guests to the main Skyline complex; from this perspective, it is possible to see across Queenstown, Lake Wakatipu, Coronet Peak, The Remarkables, Walter Peak and Cecil Peak.

The luge tracks are over 1,600 metres (5,200 feet) long. The luge contains:

- Two tracks.
- The Blue Track and Red Track.
- Ranging in steepness and corners/turns.

CORONET PEAK

Coronet Peak is a commercial ski resort located in Queenstown, New Zealand. It is situated on the southern slopes of the 1,649-meter summit, which carries its name. The resort is noted for its lengthy snow season, well-received skiing and snowboarding terrain, and lift systems.

Coronet Peak is the closest ski area to Queenstown and is open for winter and summer alpine activities. The resort offers various activities for all ages and levels, including snow sports, mountain biking, and sightseeing.

Visitors can enjoy scenic chairlifts, yooners, and snow sledges or join the Night Ski and Good Times activities.

The resort is a popular location for skiing and snowboarding enthusiasts. It offers a great range of topography with fantastic views across the Wakatipu basin. Coronet Peak is also the home of Night Ski, when the resort lights up from 4–9 pm for more skiing after the sun goes down.

Visitors can purchase lift passes, courses, equipment rentals, and transport online. The resort also offers multi-day lift pass savings, First Tracks passes, and private teaching for all ages and abilities.

Coronet Peak suits all skills, from first-timers to seasoned skiers and boarders.

The resort caters to the whole family, with kids' programs accessible for children aged five and above.

WELLINGTON

Wellington, New Zealand's capital city, is located on the southwestern tip of the North Island, between Cook Strait and the Remutaka Range. It is New Zealand's third-largest city and the administrative centre of the Wellington Region. The city is well-known for its vibrant culture, breathtaking natural beauty, and world-class cuisine.

Wellington is a little city with a fantastic mix of culture, history, nature, and gastronomy. The city has a warm marine climate and is the windiest city in the world regarding average wind speed. Discover the top ten things to do in the city, from museums and galleries to nature and wildlife, or enjoy the city's culinary and wine experiences.

The city has several attractions, including the Museum of New Zealand Te Papa Tongarewa, New Zealand's national museum and art gallery. The museum is positioned on the beach, providing visitors with a unique and exciting experience.

The Wellington Cable Car, which takes people from Lambton Quay to the Botanic Garden and offers stunning views of the city and harbor1, is another popular attraction. Wellington is also a gateway to the South Island and an ideal starting point for your tour. Visitors can take a ferry from Wellington to the South Island to enjoy the stunning Marlborough Sounds, Abel Tasman National Park, and the West Coast.

The city is also known for its vibrant nightlife, with numerous clubs, restaurants, and cafes featuring live music and entertainment. Cuba Street is a popular nightlife destination, with multiple clubs and restaurants serving a wide range of cuisine and live music.

CHRISTCHURCH

Christchurch is the largest city on New Zealand's South Island and the administrative centre of the Canterbury Region1. It is situated in Pegasus Bay on the South Island's east coast, just north of Banks Peninsula. The city is well-known for its vibrant culture, breathtaking natural beauty, and world-class cuisine.

In Christchurch, you may do everything from visiting museums and galleries to enjoying nature and wildlife. The Museum of New Zealand Te Papa Tongarewa is a must-see attraction that provides tourists with a unique and participatory experience.

The Wellington Cable Car is another popular attraction, which lifts people from Lambton Quay to the Botanic Garden and offers beautiful views of the city and harbour.

Christchurch is also a gateway to the South Island and an ideal starting point for your tour. Visitors can board a ferry from Christchurch to the South Island to explore the stunning Marlborough Sounds, Abel Tasman National Park, and the West Coast.

The city is also known for its vibrant nightlife, with numerous clubs, restaurants, and cafes featuring live music and entertainment. Cuba Street is a popular nightlife destination, with multiple clubs and restaurants serving a wide range of cuisine and live music.

ROTORUA

Rotorua is a city on New Zealand's North Island's Bay of Plenty Region1. It is famous for its spectacular geothermal landscapes, rich Mori culture, and beautiful forests.

Discover the best things to do in Rotorua, from museums and galleries to nature and animals, or enjoy the city's culinary and wine experiences.

The Museum of New Zealand Te Papa Tongarewa is a must-see attraction that provides tourists with a unique and participatory experience. The Wellington Cable Car is another popular attraction, which lifts people from Lambton Quay to the Botanic Garden and offers beautiful views of the city and harbour.

Rotorua is also a gateway to the South Island and an ideal starting point for your vacation. Visitors can take a ferry from Rotorua to the South Island to see the stunning Marlborough Sounds, Abel Tasman National Park, and the West Coast.

The city is also known for its vibrant nightlife, with numerous clubs, restaurants, and cafes featuring live music and entertainment. Cuba Street is a popular nightlife destination, with multiple clubs and restaurants serving a wide range of cuisine and live music.

WAITOMO CAVES

Waitomo Caverns is a network of caverns, sinkholes, and underground rivers in New Zealand's North Island. The caves are notable for their Arachnocampa luminosa population, a glowworm species found alone in New Zealand.

One of the most famous sights in northern New Zealand is the Waitomo Glowworm Caves.

Visitors can explore the caves and have an interactive experience with thousands of beautiful glowworms. The Legendary Black Water Rafting Co. provides the ultimate underground adventure and the most fun you'll have in the dark.

Visitors can also take a boat ride into the glowworm grotto, where they can see thousands of spectacular glowworms.

FIORDLAND NATIONAL PARK

Fiordland National Park is a protected area on New Zealand's South Island's southwest coast. It is the largest of New Zealand's 13 national parks, covering an area of 12,607 square kilometres (4,868 square miles). The park is known for its stunning ice-carved fiords, lakes, valleys, craggy granite peaks, and pristine mountain-to-sea vistas.

The park has rare vegetation and species that have existed since New Zealand was a member of the supercontinent Gondwanaland. Visitors can explore the park's fantastic collection of coves, commonly called sounds, and have a one-of-a-kind and participatory experience with thousands of spectacular glowworms.

Te Anau and Manapouri townships serve as a base for exploring Fiordland and provide various housing options, restaurants, retail, services, and activities.

THE MILFORD TRACK

The Milford Track is a 53.5-kilometer hiking trail in New Zealand's Fiordland National Park. The course is open from late October to April and is regarded as one of the most beautiful hikes in the world. The path leads you through glacier valleys, old jungles, and past flowing waterfalls.

The journey begins in Lake Te Anau and concludes at Milford Sound. The hike is classed as intermediate and takes four days to accomplish. The trail is well-kept and provides beautiful views of the surrounding area.

The trail is only accessible during the Great Walks season (October 24, 2023 - April 30, 2024). Reservations are required for huts and transportation. Outside of the Great Walks season (May 1, 2023 - October 23, 2023), only fit, experienced, and well-equipped people should try the track.

CULTURE OF MORI

Mori culture refers to the customs, cultural traditions, and beliefs of New Zealand's indigenous Mori people.

It is derived from, and still a part of, Eastern Polynesian culture. Mori culture is a distinct component of New Zealand culture that has spread worldwide due to a large diaspora and the incorporation of Mori themes into popular culture.

Mori culture is distinguished by its distinct language, extensive mythology, specific crafts, performing arts, and social structure. Te reo Mori, or Mori language, is one of New Zealand's national languages.

Mori mythology contains stories about gods and goddesses, creation, and the natural world. Mori crafts include carving, weaving, and tattooing, frequently adorned with intricate motifs and patterns.

Kapa haka, a traditional Mori dance that incorporates singing, dancing, and chanting, is one of the performing arts. Māori society is divided into **whānau** (extended families), **hapū** (sub-tribes), and **iwi** (tribes), which are all connected by **whakapapa** (genealogy).

Māori culture places a strong emphasis on manaakitanga (hospitality), Kaitiakitanga.(guardianship), and whanaungatanga (relationships).

TRANSPORTATION OPTION

New Zealand has a plethora of public transportation alternatives to select from. These include rail services from

KiwiRail, bus services for urban and rural areas, ferry services for island hopping and coastal exploration, and taxi and ride-sharing services like Uber.

Choosing transportation in New Zealand depends on how quickly you want to get from one place to the next and how much you want to see on your route. You can self-drive, join a guided tour, book flights, or take a train or bus. Passenger and vehicle ferries operate services between the North, South and other islands.

AIRPORTS

Auckland Airport (AKL): Located in Auckland, it is the largest and busiest airport in New Zealand, serving approximately 21 million people annually.

Christchurch Airport (CHC): It is the second-busiest airport in New Zealand, serving over 6.9 million passengers annually.

Wellington Airport (WLG): Located in Wellington, it is the third-busiest airport in New Zealand, serving about 4.7 million people annually.

Queenstown Airport (ZQN): Located in Queenstown, it is the fourth-busiest airport in New Zealand, servicing approximately 1.2 million people annually.

Dunedin Airport (DUD): Located in Dunedin, it is the fifth-busiest airport in New Zealand, serving about 793,000 people annually

TAXI

Taxis in New Zealand are located throughout the country and offer a comfortable and safe transport service to most destinations. You can phone a cab in New Zealand or take a taxicab from a taxi stand. Some of the most reliable and popular taxi services in New Zealand include Auckland Co-op Taxis, Corporate Cabs, Alert Taxis, Cheap Cabs, and Auckland Taxi Service.

CAR RENTALS

Some of the most trusted and popular automobile rental services in New Zealand include:

Enterprise Rent-A-Car: Offers thousands of airport and city locations near you to book a rental car with outstanding rates and service.

Turo: A vehicle-sharing marketplace allowing you to hire rental cars from reputable, local hosts near you.

KAYAK: Searches for rental vehicle deals on hundreds of car rental sites to help you find the lowest car hire.

Hertz: Offers quality automobiles accessible for rent near you with thousands of locations at airports, cities, and communities across the US and beyond.

TRAIN STATION

Some of the main railway stations in New Zealand include: Auckland Strand Station: Located in Auckland, it is the principal railway station in the city and serves as a hub for long-distance passenger trains.

Wellington Railway Station: Located in Wellington, it is the central railway station in the city and serves as a hub for long-distance passenger trains.

Christchurch Railway Station: Located in Christchurch, it is the central railway station in the city and serves as a hub for long-distance passenger trains.

Dunedin Railway Station: Located in Dunedin, it is the central railway station in the city and serves as a hub for long-distance passenger trains.

Chapter 4: Locating the Ideal Accommodations

LOCATION TO STAY

Some of the most trustworthy and famous locations to stay in New Zealand include:

1. **Novotel Auckland Airport:** A 4-star hotel located in Auckland.

2. **Crowne Plaza Auckland is an IHG Hotel:** A 4-star hotel in Auckland.

3. **Wellington:** The capital city of New Zealand, noted for its vibrant culture, magnificent natural beauty, and world-class food.

4. **Rotorua:** A city in the Bay of Plenty Region of New Zealand's North Island, famed for its breathtaking geothermal landscapes, rich Māori culture, and gorgeous woods.

5. **Christchurch**: The largest city in the South Island of New Zealand and the seat of the Canterbury Region, noted for its vibrant culture, spectacular natural beauty, and world-class food.

HOTELS

1. **Hotel St. Moritz (Queenstown):** Overlooking Lake Wakatipu, this luxury hotel in Queenstown provides lavish suites, excellent cuisine, and a spa experience. Its alpine charm and superb location make it a popular choice for discriminating guests.

2. **Hotel DeBrett (Auckland):** A boutique treasure in Auckland's city centre, Hotel DeBrett has eccentric décor, themed rooms, and a trendy bar. Its central

location gives convenient access to Auckland's cultural and entertainment attractions.

3. **The George (Christchurch):** It is a stylish boutique hotel located in Christchurch facing Hagley Park. It boasts exquisite rooms, serene grounds, and fine dining at Pescatore.

4. **Hotel Grand Windsor (Auckland):** Combining historic beauty with contemporary elegance, Hotel Grand Windsor in Auckland provides beautiful accommodations and a prime location for experiencing the city's attractions.

5. **QT Queenstown:** QT Queenstown is a trendy and stylish hotel set on the beaches of Lake Wakatipu. With a contemporary design, luxury accommodations, and stunning views, it delivers a modern and energetic atmosphere in the centre of Queenstown.

6. **The Langham, Auckland:** The Langham in Auckland is a five-star hotel offering magnificent lodgings, fine cuisine, and a wonderful spa experience. Its prominent position in Auckland's

CBD makes it a convenient alternative for business and pleasure guests.

7. **The Rees Hotel & Luxury Flats (Queenstown):** Overlooking Lake Wakatipu, The Rees Hotel offers a mix of hotel rooms and self-contained luxury flats. With beautiful vistas and a focus on customized service, it provides a calm hideaway in Queenstown.

8. **Cordis, Auckland: Cordis,** Auckland is a stylish hotel in the middle of the city. Known for its luxury lodgings, abundant dining options, and wellness facilities, it offers a sumptuous urban vacation.

9. **Te Waonui Forest Retreat (Franz Josef):** Situated in the rainforest of Franz Josef, Te Waonui Forest Retreat is an eco-friendly hotel that immerses guests in nature. With sustainable techniques, it delivers a distinctive and environmentally responsible accommodation choice.

10. **Sofitel Wellington:** Sofitel Wellington combines French grandeur with local character in the capital city. With contemporary rooms, a rooftop restaurant, and a prominent location, it offers a polished experience in the centre of Wellington.

11. **The Heritage Hotel Auckland:** The Heritage Hotel in Auckland occupies a historic building that blends classic elegance and modern luxury. It boasts ample accommodations, a rooftop pool, and easy access to Auckland's attractions.

12. **Hotel St. Moritz (Queenstown):** Overlooking Lake Wakatipu, this luxury hotel in Queenstown provides lavish suites, superb cuisine, and a spa experience. Its alpine charm and outstanding location make it a popular choice for discriminating guests.

13. **Eagles Nest (Bay of Islands):** A beachfront getaway in the Bay of Islands.

    Eagles Nest provides unique villas with private pools, individual concierge services, and spectacular views. It's a luxurious refuge for people wanting a premium experience.

14. **The Lodge at Kauri Cliffs (Northland):** Set against the Northland environment, this alpine getaway includes a world-class golf course, spa, and sumptuous accommodations. The Lodge at Kauri Cliffs gives a beautiful getaway amidst nature.

15. **Millbrook Resort (Queenstown):** Nestled in the Southern Alps, Millbrook Resort offers upmarket amenities, award-winning golf courses, and a quiet location. It's a great blend of mountain beauty and modern luxury.

16. **Blanket Bay (Glenorchy):** Situated in Glenorchy, Blanket Bay offers a quiet alpine getaway with rustic elegance. Guests can enjoy magnificent rooms, excellent restaurants, and outdoor activities surrounded by the Southern Alps.

17. **Hapuku Lodge + Tree Houses (Kaikoura):** Set in Kaikoura, this lodge provides luxury suites and unique treehouse accommodations on a thriving deer farm. Hapuku Lodge combines sustainability with elegance amid spectacular coastline views.

RESORTS

1. **Huka Lodge (Taupo):**

Nestled along the banks of the Waikato River in Taupo, Huka Lodge is a renowned luxury retreat. Surrounded by pure nature, it provides premium rooms, excellent restaurants, and outdoor activities in a serene location.

2. Kauri Cliffs (Northland):

Located in Northland, Kauri Cliffs is a premier golf and spa resort. The resort boasts a world-class golf course, sumptuous accommodations, and abundant spa amenities amid stunning settings.

3. MATAKAURI LODGE (QUEENSTOWN):

Overlooking Lake Wakatipu near Queenstown, Matakauri Lodge is a luxury getaway. With contemporary design, spacious apartments, and spectacular lake views, it gives a quiet respite in the Southern Alps.

4. Solitaire Lodge (Rotorua):

Situated on the beaches of Lake Tarawera in Rotorua, Solitaire Lodge offers a private and elegant experience. Guests can enjoy well-appointed accommodations, excellent dining, and panoramic views of the lake and volcanic mountains.

5. Cape Kidnappers (Hawke's Bay):

Perched on the cliffs of Hawke's Bay, Cape Kidnappers is a luxury lodge and golf resort. Known for its breathtaking vistas, world-class golf course, and luxury rooms, it gives a refuge in a seaside paradise.

6. Bay of Many Coves Resort (Marlborough Sounds):

Accessible only by boat in the Marlborough Sounds, Bay of Many Coves Resort offers a private hideaway. With beachfront villas, great restaurants, and outdoor activities, it gives a magnificent shelter surrounded by nature.

7. Hapuku Lodge + Tree Houses (Kaikoura):

Besides offering unusual treehouse rooms, Hapuku Resort in Kaikoura is a resort and restaurant focusing on sustainability. Guests can enjoy eco-friendly luxury amidst the gorgeous seaside scenery.

8. Azur Lodge (Queenstown):

Overlooking Lake Wakatipu in Queenstown, Azur Lodge provides individual villas with spectacular views. Known for its customized service and contemporary decor, it offers a private and romantic escape.

9. Wharekauhau Country Estate (Wairarapa):

Wharekauhau Country Estate is a magnificent resort set on a 5,500-acre working sheep and cattle farm located in the Wairarapa region. Guests can enjoy luxurious lodgings, farm-to-table dining, and various outdoor activities.

10. Fiordland Lodge (Te Anau):

Perched on a hill overlooking Lake Te Anau, Fiordland Lodge is a luxury getaway in the Fiordland region. With stylish rooms, superb dining, and easy access to Fiordland National Park, it provides tranquil respite in a UNESCO World Heritage location.

11. Split Apple Retreat (Abel Tasman):

Situated near Abel Tasman National Park, Split Apple Retreat is a wellness and luxury retreat. Offering ocean views, spa facilities, and holistic health programs gives a revitalizing vacation in a coastal paradise.

12. Poronui (Taupo):

In the Kaimanawa Ranges foothills, Poronui is a luxurious wilderness getaway near Taupo. Guests can experience luxurious lodgings, fly-fishing, and outdoor excursions in a quiet and pristine area.

13. The Farm at Cape Kidnappers (Hawke's Bay):

The Farm at Cape Kidnappers is a premium lodge and golf facility in Hawke's Bay. Set on a 6,000-acre farm, it provides magnificent vistas, a world-class golf course, and luxurious lodgings.

14. Te Waonui Forest Retreat (Franz Josef):

Te Waonui Forest Retreat is an eco-friendly retreat located in the jungle near Franz Josef Glacier. Guests can experience sustainable luxury, wellness facilities, and convenient access to the natural beauties of the West Coast.

15. Sofitel Queenstown Hotel & Spa:

Situated in the heart of Queenstown, Sofitel Queenstown Hotel & Spa mixes French grandeur with local character. With sumptuous accommodations, a spa, and closeness to Queenstown's attractions, it offers a refined urban escape.

CAMPING SITES

1. Department of Conservation (DOC) Campsites:

The Department of Conservation operates a network of campsites throughout New Zealand, offering a range of camping experiences. From coastal sites to those tucked in native bush, DOC campsites give an authentic and economical opportunity to interact with nature.

2. Top 10 Holiday Parks (Various Locations):

Top 10 Holiday Parks are a series of New Zealand campgrounds offering various services such as powered sites, cabins, and communal amenities. These parks cater to campers, caravaners, and those wanting a family-friendly camping experience.

3. Freedom Camping Sites:

New Zealand allows freedom camping in specific places for self-contained vehicles. These places provide an opportunity to camp in picturesque locations, frequently near beaches or natural attractions. It's crucial to comply with local standards and ensure your car is self-contained.

4. Glamping Hub (Nationwide):

For those seeking a more elegant camping experience, Glamping Hub offers distinctive and pleasant accommodations across New Zealand. From luxury tents to modest cabins, glamping adds a touch of comfort in stunning settings.

5. Camping Grounds in Fiordland National Park:

Fiordland National Park, with its spectacular fjords and landscapes, offers camping grounds in locations such as Milford Sound and Doubtful Sound. These campsites allow you to immerse yourself in the wildness of the South Island.

6. Waitomo Top 10 Holiday Park (Waitomo Caves):

Located near the famous Waitomo Caves, this vacation park offers camping amenities and is perfect for visiting the caves and the surrounding glowworm-filled surroundings.

7. Lake Taupo TOP 10 Holiday Resort:

Situated near the beaches of Lake Taupo, this holiday resort has camping spots with spectacular views. It's excellent for water sports and touring the Central North Island.

8. Mount Cook Village Campground (Aoraki / Mount Cook):

Nestled in the shadow of Aoraki / Mount Cook, this campground offers a unique camping experience surrounded by the Southern Alps. It's a perfect base for experiencing the alpine splendour of the Aoraki region.

9. Abel Tasman National Park Campsites:

Abel Tasman National Park on the South Island offers various campsites along its gorgeous coastal trail. Campers can enjoy oceanfront sites surrounded by golden sands and natural flora, creating a unique coastal camping experience.

10. Mavora Lakes Campsite (Southland):

Located in the Southland region, Mavora Lakes Campsite is set between calm lakes and mountain views. It's a quiet site for camping, fishing, and experiencing the area's natural beauty.

11. Lake Pukaki Freedom Camping Area (Canterbury):

Along the shores of Lake Pukaki, this freedom camping place affords stunning views of the blue lake and the Southern Alps. It's a fantastic site for stargazing and admiring the alpine vistas.

12. Kaiteriteri Beach Motor Camp (Nelson):

Situated near Kaiteriteri Beach, this motor park offers camping spots with convenient access to the golden sands and crystal-clear waters. It's a popular alternative for those exploring the Abel Tasman region.

13. Purakaunui Bay Campsite (Otago):

Found on the Otago coast, Purakaunui Bay Campsite offers a lovely environment with coastal cliffs and a sandy beach. It's a peaceful area for camping, seaside hikes, and birdwatching.

14. Hanmer Springs TOP 10 Holiday Park (Canterbury):

Located near the famed Hanmer Springs thermal spas, this holiday park provides camping amenities surrounded by mountain scenery. It's a perfect base for visiting the mountain community and its natural hot springs.

15. Lake Tekapo Motels & Holiday Park:

With views of the famed Lake Tekapo and the Southern Alps, this holiday park offers camping spots in a lovely alpine location. Visitors can enjoy the turquoise waters of the lake and the nearby Church of the Good Shepherd.

HOSTELS

1. YHA New Zealand (Various Locations):

YHA New Zealand is a well-known network of hostels with locations across the country. These hostels are noted for their budget-friendly rooms, communal environment, and facilities appealing to tourists of all ages.

2. Nomads Queenstown Hostel (Queenstown):

Nomads Queenstown Hostel is centrally located in Queenstown and offers budget-friendly dormitory-style and private room accommodations. With a bustling environment, it's a popular choice for backpackers experiencing the adventure capital of New Zealand.

3. Haka Lodge (Various Locations):

Haka Lodge is a hostel chain located in significant destinations like Queenstown, Christchurch, and Auckland.

The hostels mix trendy design with affordability, creating a comfortable and friendly tourist environment.

4. Bamber House (Auckland):

Bamber House is a historic hostel in Auckland housed in a lovely Edwardian home. It offers budget-friendly dormitory and private room options, blending a homely ambience with a handy location in the centre of Auckland.

5. The Wellington (Wellington):

The Wellington is a modern hostel located in Wellington, the capital city. With a focus on sustainability, it provides eco-friendly lodgings in dormitories and individual rooms, making it a popular choice for budget-conscious guests.

6. Kiwi Experience Hostel (Rotorua):

Kiwi Experience Hostel in Rotorua is part of the famous Kiwi Experience travel network. The hostel offers inexpensive lodgings and a convivial ambience, especially to travellers enjoying the thermal marvels of Rotorua.

7. Base Backpackers Taupo (Taupo):

Base Backpackers in Taupo is situated near the shores of Lake Taupo. The hostel features a lively environment, budget-friendly dormitories, and private rooms, making it a perfect location for touring the Central North Island.

8. Adventure Queenstown Hostel (Queenstown):

Adventure Queenstown Hostel is located in the centre of Queenstown and offers cheap rooms for adventure activities. It's a popular alternative for individuals wanting an exciting and social hostel experience.

9. Haka Lodge Christchurch (Christchurch):

Haka Lodge Christchurch is part of the Haka Lodge chain and is located in the dynamic city of Christchurch. Known for its modern architecture and friendly atmosphere, the hostel provides a pleasant base for touring South Island's major metropolises.

10. The Bug Backpackers (Nelson):

The Bug Backpackers is in the picturesque city of Nelson and offers budget-friendly accommodations with a pleasant and laid-back attitude. The hostel provides a convenient location for exploring the Nelson region and its cultural community.

11. Sir Cedrics Tahuna Pod Hostel (Queenstown):

Sir Cedrics Tahuna Pod Hostel in Queenstown offers a unique accommodation experience with pod-style beds. This hostel mixes modern design with affordability, creating a comfortable and social setting for travellers in the adventure capital.

12. YHA Franz Josef (Franz Josef):

YHA Franz Josef is located in the West Coast's scenic Franz Josef Glacier area. The hostel offers budget-friendly lodgings, including dormitory and private rooms, making it an excellent location for exploring the glacier and its surroundings.

13. The Attic Backpackers (Dunedin):

The Attic Backpackers is housed in a historic building in Dunedin. Known for its welcoming atmosphere and strategic location, the hostel delivers a distinctive and characterful experience for guests experiencing the Otago region.

14. Jailhouse Accommodation (Christchurch):

Jailhouse Accommodation in Christchurch is housed in a former jail structure, providing a unique and historic hostel experience. The hostel mixes budget-friendly rooms with a unique peek into New Zealand's past.

15. Adventure Q2 Hostel (Queenstown):

Adventure Q2 Hostel in Queenstown is noted for its central location and friendly environment. With budget-friendly accommodations, it caters to guests wishing to experience the excitement of adventure activities in the Queenstown region.

CABINS AND VACATION RENTALS

1. **Fiordland Lodge Cabins (Te Anau):**

Fiordland Lodge offers beautiful cottages overlooking Lake Te Anau. Nestled in the Fiordland region, these cottages provide a private refuge with stunning views of the mountains and lake.

2. **Arrowtown Born of Gold Holiday Park Cabins (Arrowtown):**

Located in the historic village of Arrowtown, this holiday park offers cosy cabins amidst the breathtaking landscapes of the Southern Alps. It's a perfect location for experiencing Arrowtown's gold mining history and the neighbouring Queenstown region.

3. **Golden Bay Hideaway (Takaka):**

Golden Bay Hideaway offers unique holiday rentals, including cabins and eco-friendly cottages. Set near Golden Bay, these lodgings give a calm and sustainable vacation surrounded by native flora.

4. Wharepuke Subtropical Accommodation (Kerikeri):

Wharepuke Subtropical Accommodation in Kerikeri offers self-contained cottages nestled within subtropical gardens. These unique cottages give a calm and creative refuge in the Northland region.

5. Lake Tekapo Cottages (Lake Tekapo):

Lake Tekapo Cottages provides lovely self-contained accommodations near the turquoise waters of Lake Tekapo. With a blend of modern and rustic appeal, these cottages offer a pleasant base for exploring the Mackenzie region.

6. Wanaka Kiwi Holiday Park & Motels Cabins (Wanaka):

Wanaka Kiwi Holiday Park offers a selection of lodgings, including cabins, in the picturesque town of Wanaka. Surrounded by mountains and near Lake Wanaka, these cabins give a convenient and economical stay.

7. The Barn Glamping (Raglan):

The Barn in Raglan offers glamping lodgings in a contemporary and rustic setting. With distinctive cottages and tents, it gives a boutique camping experience near Raglan's famous surf beaches.

8. Punakaiki Forest Retreat (Punakaiki):

Punakaiki Forest Retreat offers eco-friendly bungalows in the lush woods near Punakaiki. These quiet cabins provide a peaceful vacation close to the Pancake Rocks and other West Coast attractions.

9. Pohara Beach TOP 10 Holiday Park Cabins (Golden Bay):

Pohara Beach TOP 10 Holiday Park offers lovely accommodations in Golden Bay with beachfront access. These cottages provide a comfortable location for enjoying the Tasman region's sun, surf, and sand.

10. Mahu Whenua Ridgeline Homestead & Eco Sanctuary (Wanaka):

Mahu Whenua offers a magnificent homestead and environmental retreat near Wanaka. With exclusive holiday properties, including a breathtaking hilltop homestead, it provides a high-end and secluded escape amidst the Southern Alps.

11. Omaha Beach Holiday Park Cabins (Omaha):

Omaha Beach Holiday Park offers chalets in a beachfront location near Auckland. Ideal for beach enthusiasts, these cabins give a convenient base for visiting the Omaha Beach region and adjacent vineyards.

12. Tongariro Holiday Park Cabins (Turangi):

Tongariro Holiday Park has cottages near the Tongariro National Park. Set in the centre of North Island, these cabins offer a comfortable stay for guests visiting the neighbouring mountains, lakes, and hiking trails.

13. Mountain Range Boutique Lodge (Hanmer Springs):

Mountain Range Boutique Lodge offers individual cabins with alpine views near Hanmer Springs. These elegant cottages provide a pleasant and serene retreat in the Canterbury region.

14. Flock Hill Lodge Cabins (Arthur's Pass):

Flock Hill Lodge offers accommodations near Arthur's Pass in the Southern Alps. Set in a high-country station, these cottages give a rustic and charming getaway surrounded by mountains and panoramic landscapes.

15. Lake Hawea Holiday Park Cabins (Lake Hawea):

Lake Hawea Holiday Park offers accommodations with views of Lake Hawea in the Otago area. These cabins provide a calm lakeside refuge for those seeking a tranquil holiday.

BED AND BREAKFAST

1. Hulbert House (Queenstown):

Hulbert House is a luxurious Bed & Breakfast in Queenstown. Set in a Victorian home with spectacular lake views, it provides elegant accommodations, individual service, and a delicious breakfast.

2. Greenhill Lodge (Hawke's Bay):

Greenhill Lodge is a historic B&B near Hastings in Hawke's Bay. Surrounded by gardens and vineyards, it provides a serene vacation with well-appointed accommodations and a concentration on gourmet cuisine.

3. Kauri Villas (Whangaroa):

Kauri Villas is a B&B in the Northland region, offering a blend of Victorian beauty and modern luxury. It is set in a subtropical garden and provides a quiet refuge near the Whangaroa Harbour.

4. The Boatshed (Waiheke Island):

The Boatshed on Waiheke Island is a boutique B&B with nautical-inspired decor. Overlooking the Hauraki Gulf, it offers modern accommodations, a waterfront setting, and a superb breakfast.

5. Pen-y-Bryn Lodge (Oamaru):

Pen-y-Bryn Lodge is a Victorian mansion B&B in Oamaru. Known for its heritage charm, antiques, and gourmet breakfasts, it delivers an elegant stay in the Otago region.

6. Acorns Wellington Bed and Breakfast:

Acorns Wellington is a B&B housed in a Victorian villa in the heart of Wellington. With spacious rooms and a central location, it's an excellent alternative for touring the capital city.

7. Tin Dragon Trail Cottages (St. Bathans):

Tin Dragon Trail Cottages offer B&B accommodations in the ancient village of St. Bathans in Central Otago. The cottages give a cosy and charming vacation near Blue Lake.

8. The Red Barn (Cambridge):

The Red Barn is a B&B in Cambridge, Waikato, built in a renovated barn with modern conveniences. Gardens and fields surround it, offering a serene hideaway on the North Island.

9. Chalet Romantica (Hanmer Springs):

Chalet Romantica is a B&B in Hanmer Springs recognized for its Alpine beauty and romantic setting. With modest accommodations, mountain views, and a hot tub, it provides a tranquil hideaway in the Canterbury region.

10. Pacific View Paradise Bed & Breakfast (Tutukaka):

Pacific View Paradise is a B&B overlooking the Tutukaka Coast. With breathtaking ocean views, luxurious lodgings, and a welcoming ambience, it offers a coastal retreat in Northland.

11. Browns Boutique Hotel (Queenstown):

Browns Boutique Hotel is a historic B&B in the heart of Queenstown. It is set in a Victorian home and offers boutique-style rooms, individual service, and easy access to Queenstown's attractions.

12. Vintners Retreat (Marlborough):

Vintners Retreat is a luxurious B&B in Marlborough, surrounded by vineyards. The spacious villas provide a calm location, and guests may enjoy the region's renowned wines and food.

13. Wanaka Haven (Wanaka):

Wanaka Haven is a B&B nestled in a beautiful environment near Lake Wanaka. With modern architecture, sophisticated décor, and mountain vistas, it offers a magnificent hideaway in the Southern Alps.

14. The Dairy Private Luxury Hotel (Queenstown):

The Dairy Private Luxury Hotel is a B&B in Queenstown that offers boutique lodgings in a former dairy. With a mix of historic charm and contemporary elegance, it gives a unique stay in the adventure capital.

15. Canterbury House Boutique Bed & Breakfast (Christchurch):

Canterbury House is a small B&B in Christchurch, housed in a heritage-listed farmstead. With magnificent accommodations, gorgeous grounds, and a strategic position, it offers a refined stay on the South Island.

ITINERARY

DAY 1

THRILLING WATER ADVENTURES

Morning. Start your day with a delicious breakfast at

Orphans Kitchen and fuel up for an exciting day ahead.

After breakfast, embark on the **Te Awa Kairangi Grade 3 Wilderness Whitewater Duckie Tour**, where you'll navigate through thrilling rapids and enjoy the stunning wilderness scenery.

Afternoon. For lunch, head to **Federal Delicatessen** and indulge in their mouthwatering sandwiches and deli-style dishes. After lunch, continue your water adventures with the **Te Awa Kairangi Grade 2 Scenic Rafting Tour**, a more relaxed rafting experience that offers beautiful scenic views.

Evening. Treat yourself to a delicious dinner at **Wu & You**, known for its Asian fusion cuisine.

Enjoy a variety of flavours and unique dishes in a vibrant atmosphere.

DAY 2

EXPLORING THE CITY

Morning. Start your day with a visit to the iconic **Wellington Te Awa Kairangi Class 3 Whitewater Rafting Tour**. Get your adrenaline pumping as you navigate through challenging rapids. Afterwards, grab a quick bite at **Gusto at the Grand** for a tasty brunch.

Afternoon. Explore the city's vibrant culinary scene with a food tour. Visit **Depot, Cazador**, and **Ortega Fish Shack & Bar** to savour a variety of flavours and dishes. Don't miss the opportunity to try some local seafood specialities.

Evening. End your day with a delightful dinner at **Giraffe**, known for its modern New Zealand cuisine. Enjoy a cosy and intimate dining experience with delicious dishes made from locally sourced ingredients.

DAY 3
URBAN DELIGHTS

Morning. Start your day in Auckland with a visit to **the New Zealand eSIM Data Plan** to ensure you stay connected throughout your trip. Afterwards, grab a coffee at **Baduzzi** and enjoy the scenic views of the city.

Afternoon. Explore the vibrant food scene of Auckland with a visit to **Gatherings**, **Cassia**, and **Coco's Cantina**. Indulge in a variety of cuisines and flavours, from modern New Zealand dishes to Indian-inspired creations.

Evening. Enjoy a delicious dinner at **Ostro**, a waterfront restaurant known for its fresh seafood and stunning views. After dinner, head to **Lake Bar** for some drinks and live music.

DAY 4
ADVENTURE CAPITAL

Morning. Start your day with a scenic drive to Queenstown. Once you arrive, grab a quick breakfast at **Mudbrick Vineyard and Restaurant** and fuel up for a day of adventure.

fternoon. Experience the thrill of **Te Awa Kairangi Grade 2 Scenic Duckie Tour**, where you'll navigate the scenic rivers of Queenstown in inflatable kayaks. Afterwards, enjoy a delicious lunch at **The Meat & Wine Co** and savour their mouthwatering steaks.

Evening. For dinner, head to **Cable Bay Vineyards** and enjoy a delightful meal paired with their exquisite wines. End your day with a visit to **Ponsonby Central**, a lively food and entertainment hub where you can enjoy drinks and live music.

DAY 5
SCENIC BEAUTY

Morning. Start your day with a visit to **New Zealand eSIM Data Plan** to ensure you stay connected throughout your trip. Afterwards, grab a quick breakfast at **Cibo** and enjoy the beautiful views of Queenstown.

Afternoon. Explore the stunning landscapes of Queenstown with a visit to **Wellington Te Awa Kairangi Class 3 Whitewater Rafting Tour**. Experience the thrill of whitewater rafting while surrounded by the breathtaking beauty of nature. For lunch, head to **The Grove** and enjoy their delicious seasonal dishes.

Evening. End your trip with a memorable dinner at **Provenance of Auckland**, a restaurant known for its farm-to-table concept and dedication to locally sourced ingredients. Savour the flavours of New Zealand in a cosy and inviting atmosphere.

Chapter 5: Exploring New Zealand's Wonders

SIGHTSEEING.

NORTH ISLAND:

1. Fiordland National Park and Milford Sound:

A World Heritage Site, Fiordland National Park protects some of the most magnificent scenery in the country. Glaciers shaped this stunning landscape, cutting the famous fjords of Milford, Dusky, and Doubtful Sounds. Visitors here can experience gushing cascades, offshore islands, virgin rain forests, enormous lakes, and jagged mountain summits. Not unexpectedly, the park is a sanctuary for hikers with some of the country's best hiking, including the famous Milford Track.

2. Bay of Islands:

A three-hour journey north of Auckland, the gorgeous Bay of Islands is one of the most popular vacation locations in the country. More than 144 islands dot the dazzling water, making it a sanctuary for sailing and yachting. Penguins, dolphins, whales, and marlin reside in these lush waters, and the location is a favourite sport-fishing spot. Visitors can water kayak along the coast, trek the many island trails, bask in peaceful bays, tour Cape Brett and the iconic rock formation called Hole in the Rock, and discover subtropical forests where Kauri trees flourish. The small villages in the surrounding area, such as Russell, Opua, Paihia, and Kerikeri, are beautiful locations for exploring this picturesque bay.

3. Museum of New Zealand Te Papa Tongarewa:

Located in Wellington, the museum is the National Museum and Art Gallery of New Zealand. It offers tourists a unique and engaging experience, including displays of the country's natural history, Māori culture, and art. The museum also boasts a significant collection of antiquities from around the world.

4. Auckland War Memorial Museum:

Located in Auckland, the museum is an excellent site to learn about New Zealand's history and culture. It exhibits the country's natural heritage, Māori culture, and military history. The museum also features a planetarium and a significant collection of antiquities worldwide.

5. Waitangi Treaty Grounds (Paihia, Northland):
The place where the Maori leaders signed an agreement with officials of the British crown, surrendering sovereignty of their territory.

6. Rotorua Redwoods Forest (Rotorua, Bay of Plenty):
Explore the towering Redwoods Forest in Rotorua, offering scenic walking and mountain biking paths.

7. Weta Workshop (Wellington):
Visit the Weta Workshop in Wellington, which is recognized for its contributions to film special effects, notably "The Lord of the Rings."

8. Cape Reinga (Northland): Cape Reinga is the northernmost extremity of New Zealand, where the Tasman Sea and the Pacific Ocean meet, affording beautiful coastal vistas.

9. Napier's Art Deco Architecture (Hawke's Bay):

Take a trip through Napier to see its well-preserved Art Deco buildings, a product of rebuilding after the 1931 earthquake.

10. Hobbiton Movie Set (Matamata, Waikato):

In the Waikato region, Matamata is home to the Hobbiton Movie Set, a must-visit for fans of "The Lord of the Rings" and "The Hobbit" trilogies.

11. Waitomo Glowworm Caves (Waitomo, Waikato):

Explore the spectacular Waitomo Glowworm Caves, situated in the Waikato region. The caves are famed for their stunning glowworm displays.

12. Tongariro Alpine Crossing (Tongariro National Park, Central North Island):

The Tongariro Alpine Crossing is a demanding journey in the volcanic landscapes of Tongariro National Park.

13. Te Puia (Rotorua, Bay of Plenty):

Rotorua in the Bay of Plenty is home to Te Puia, featuring geothermal wonders, Maori culture, and the famed Pohutu Geyser.

14. Wai-O-Tapu Thermal Wonderland (Rotorua, Bay of Plenty):

Also in Rotorua, Wai-O-Tapu Thermal Wonderland has multicolored thermal pools and fascinating geothermal landforms.

15. Auckland Sky Tower (Auckland):

Auckland's landmark Sky Tower affords panoramic views of the city and the surrounding surroundings.

SOUTH ISLAND:

16. Queenstown and Lake Wakatipu:

Snuggled between the shores of dazzling Lake Wakatipu and the snowy peaks of the Remarkables, Queenstown is New Zealand's adventure capital and one of the country's top locations for international visitors. The town's natural beauty and proximity to outdoor adventure destinations like the Milford Sound, the Remarkables, and Mount Aspiring National Park make it popular for thrill-seekers and nature enthusiasts.

17. Lake Wanaka (Otago):

Enjoy the calm of Lake Wanaka, surrounded by mountains, and visit the famed Wanaka Tree.

The Catlins (Southland):

Explore the rugged beauty of The Catlins in Southland, noted for its waterfalls, coastal cliffs, and rich fauna.

18. Kaikoura (Canterbury):

In the Canterbury region, Kaikoura offers the opportunity to watch whales and swim with dolphins.

Dunedin's Baldwin Street (Otago):

Visit Baldwin Street in Dunedin, which is recognized as the world's steepest residential street.

19. Lake Pukaki (Canterbury):

Marvel at the turquoise waters of Lake Pukaki, with vistas of Aoraki / Mount Cook in the distance.

20. Otago Rail Trail (Otago):

Cycle or stroll the Otago Rail Trail, a picturesque path across Central Otago displaying ancient gold-mining landscapes.

21. Farewell Spit (Tasman):

Explore Farewell Spit, a natural sand spit in Golden Bay with distinctive birds and coastal beauty.

22. Marlborough Sounds (Marlborough):

Cruise through the gorgeous Marlborough Sounds, a network of sea-drowned valleys famous for their beauty.

23. Whanganui River (Manawatu-Whanganui):

Take a lovely drive on the Whanganui River, noted for its lush surroundings and the ancient Whanganui River Road.

24. Aoraki / Mount Cook National Park (Canterbury):

Aoraki / Mount Cook National Park in the Canterbury region is home to New Zealand's tallest mountain and spectacular alpine landscapes.

25. Abel Tasman National Park (Nelson-Tasman):

Nelson-Tasman is the gateway to Abel Tasman National Park, famed for its golden beaches, coastal footpaths, and kayaking options.

26. Lake Tekapo and Church of the Good Shepherd (Mackenzie):

The turquoise waters of Lake Tekapo and the renowned Church of the Good Shepherd are located in the Mackenzie region.

27. Fox and Franz Josef Glaciers (West Coast):

Explore the West Coast to observe the spectacular Fox and Franz Josef Glaciers.

28. Punakaiki Pancake Rocks (Punakaiki, West Coast):

Punakaiki on the West Coast is notable for its Pancake Rocks and Blowholes, a unique geological structure.

29. Dunedin and Otago Peninsula (Otago):

Dunedin in the Otago region is a historic city, and the Otago Peninsula offers animal encounters with albatross and penguins.

ANCIENT MONUMENTS AND HISTORIC SITES

NORTH ISLAND:

1. TE WAIMATE MISSION (WAIMATE NORTH, NORTHLAND):

This mission station dates back to the early 19th century and provides an insight into missionary life.

2. BURIED VILLAGE OF TE WAIROA (ROTORUA, BAY OF PLENTY):

Te Wairoa was buried by the eruption of Mount Tarawera in 1886. The site has been largely excavated, revealing the relics of a 19th-century Maori settlement and Victorian tourists.

3. ST. MARY'S CHURCH (TARANAKI):

St. Mary's is a lovely stone church in New Plymouth, erected in the 1840s. It's one of the oldest stone churches in New Zealand.

4. ZEALANDIA (WELLINGTON):

Zealandia is a revolutionary eco-sanctuary focusing on local wildlife protection. It provides an insight into New Zealand's natural history and the current attempts to safeguard its distinctive flora and animals.

5. STONE STORE (KERIKERI, NORTHLAND):

The Stone Store at Kerikeri, besides being one of the oldest buildings, is part of the Kerikeri Mission Station, showing missionary history and early encounters between Maori and Europeans.

SOUTH ISLAND:

6. OTAGO PENINSULA FORTS (OTAGO):

Explore ruins of old forts on the Otago Peninsula, built during the mid-19th century as a defence system against prospective attackers.

7. POMPALLIER MISSION AND PRINTERY (RUSSELL, NORTHLAND):

Pompallier Mission, built in the 1840s, is a French Catholic mission with a printing press used to create holy writings in Maori.

8. ARROWTOWN (OTAGO):

This ancient gold-mining town has kept its 19th-century architecture, allowing a glimpse into the gold rush era.

9. AKAROA LIGHTHOUSE (CANTERBURY):

The Akaroa Lighthouse, completed in 1880, is a historic nautical structure with panoramic port views.

10. OLVESTON HISTORIC HOME (DUNEDIN, OTAGO):

Olveston is a wonderfully restored historic property in Dunedin, allowing a peek into the lifestyle of a wealthy family in the early 20th century.

11. SCOTT'S HUT, ANTARCTIC CENTRE (CHRISTCHURCH):

While not old, Scott's Hut is a reproduction of the base established by Captain Robert Falcon Scott during his Antarctic explorations. It's part of the Antarctic Centre in Christchurch

BOTH ISLANDS:

12. STONE STORE (KERIKERI, NORTHLAND):

The Stone Store at Kerikeri is one of New Zealand's oldest buildings, dating back to the early 19th century. It acted as a store for mission materials.

13. OLD ST. PAUL'S (WELLINGTON):

While not ancient by worldwide standards, Old St. Paul's is a wooden church in Wellington dating back to the 19th century, notable for its Gothic-revival architecture.

14. WAIRAU BAR ARCHAEOLOGICAL SITE (MARLBOROUGH):

Wairau Bar is an important archaeological site, giving evidence of early Polynesian settlement in New Zealand.

15. STONEHENGE AOTEAROA (WAIRARAPA):

While a modern invention, Stonehenge Aotearoa in Wairarapa is a stone circle and astronomical observatory inspired by ancient locations.

16. CANTERBURY MUSEUM (CHRISTCHURCH):

Canterbury Museum in Christchurch includes extensive collections showcasing the natural and human history of New Zealand, including Maori relics and Antarctic exploration exhibits.

17. THE ARTS CENTRE (CHRISTCHURCH):

The Arts Centre in Christchurch, based in Gothic Revival buildings, focuses on cultural and creative activity of historical significance.

18. WELLINGTON CABLE CAR (WELLINGTON):

While not an old site, the Wellington Cable Car has been a part of the city's history since 1902, giving panoramic views and connecting the city to the Botanic Garden.

MAORI CULTURAL SITES:

19. PUKETAPU PA SITE (HAWKE'S BAY):

Puketapu Pa is a historic Maori fortification with terraced earthworks, allowing a peek into the early settlement patterns of the Maori people.

20. BIRCHWOOD WALLS (NORTHLAND):

These ancient pa sites in Northland include defensive earthworks created by the Maori people.

21. NGARUAWAHIA (WAIKATO):

Ngaruawahia is a crucial venue for the Maori King Movement, with Turangawaewae Marae serving as a central gathering place.

22. OHAEAWAI PA (NORTHLAND):

Ohaeawai Pa was a significant battleground during the Northern War in 1845. The earthworks and tunnels are still evident today.

23. TAMAKI MAORI VILLAGE (ROTORUA, BAY OF PLENTY):

Tamaki Maori Village offers an authentic cultural experience, displaying traditional Maori rituals, performances, and a recreated village.

24. TE AWAHOU NIEUWE STROOM (FOXTON, MANAWATU-WHANGANUI):

This cultural and community centre honours the history and culture of the region's Maori, Dutch, and other cultures.

NATURAL WONDERS

1. **Waitomo Caves:** A network of underground caves in the Waikato Region, roughly 200 kilometres from Auckland. The caves are famed for their glowworms and underground boat rides.

2. **Tongariro Alpine Crossing:** A 19.4-kilometer hiking track that traverses through the Tongariro National Park, a UNESCO World Heritage Site. The walk offers beautiful views of volcanic mountains, alpine meadows, and green lakes.

3. **Franz Josef Glacier:** A glacier found in Westland Tai Poutini National Park on the West Coast of New Zealand's South Island. Guided glacier tours give excellent views of the surrounding mountains and valleys.

4. **Milford Sound:** A fjord located in Fiordland National Park, famed for its stunning landscape and waterfalls. Visitors can take a boat tour of the fjord to enjoy its splendour up close.

5. **Haast Pass Blue waters:** A series of crystal-clear waters located in the Haast Pass, a mountain pass in the Southern Alps of New Zealand. The pools are a popular area for swimming and picnicking.

6. **Pupu Springs:** New Zealand's most incredible freshwater springs are located in Golden Bay. The springs are famed for their crystal-clear waters and native flora.

7. **Pancake Rocks**: A rock formation located on the West Coast of the South Island. The rocks are named for their unusual layered look, resembling a pancake stack.

8. **Mount Aspiring National Park:** A national park in the Southern Alps of New Zealand. The park is home to various landscapes, including glaciers, alpine meadows, and woods.

9. **Lake Tekapo:** A glacial lake in the Mackenzie Basin of New Zealand's South Island. The lake is recognized for its turquoise colour and spectacular views of the surrounding mountains.

10. **Abel Tasman National Park:** A national park located near the northern end of New Zealand's South Island. The park is famed for its golden beaches, crystal-clear waters, and coastal woodlands.

MUSEUMS

NORTH ISLAND:

1. Te Papa Tongarewa – Museum of New Zealand (Wellington):

New Zealand's national museum features different displays of Maori culture, natural history, and modern art.

2. Auckland War Memorial Museum (Auckland):

A comprehensive museum spanning military history, environmental history, and Maori and Pacific Island culture.

Canterbury Museum (Christchurch):

It is located in Christchurch and offers displays of the region's natural history, Antarctic expeditions, and Maori artefacts.

3. Rotorua Museum Te Whare Taonga o Te Arawa (Rotorua):

Housed in a historic bathhouse, it exhibits Rotorua's Maori culture, geothermal attractions, and local history.

4. Whanganui Regional Museum (Whanganui):

We are showcasing the natural and cultural history of the Whanganui region, including Maori taonga (treasures).

SOUTH ISLAND:

5. Otago Museum (Dunedin):

It covers natural history, cultural relics, and science, concentrating on Otago and the wider Pacific region.

6. Southland Museum and Art Gallery (Invercargill):

Known for its tuatara enclosure and exhibitions on Southland's natural and cultural history.

7. Marlborough Museum (Blenheim):

Explores the Marlborough region's history, art, and culture, including Maori and European heritage.

8. Waikato Museum Te Whare Taonga o Waikato (Hamilton):

Features exhibits about Waikato's cultural and ecological past and modern art.

BOTH ISLANDS:

9. Museum of Transport and Technology (MOTAT) (Auckland):

Showcases New Zealand's transportation and technical heritage through interactive exhibits.

10. New Zealand Maritime Museum (Auckland):

Focuses on New Zealand's marine heritage, featuring displays on exploration and sailing history.

11. The Dowse Art Museum (Lower Hutt):

A contemporary art museum presenting a varied spectrum of New Zealand and foreign art.

12. MTG Hawke's Bay (Napier):

Merges a museum, theatre, and gallery, presenting Hawke's Bay's art, culture, and history.

13. Nelson Provincial Museum (Nelson):

Highlights Nelson's history, Maori relics, and natural heritage, especially the iconic Boulder Bank.

Rotorua Arts Village (Rotorua):

A nexus for the arts, with galleries, studios, and exhibits exhibiting local and national artists.

14. Tairawhiti Museum (Gisborne):

Explores the cultural and historical heritage of the Gisborne region, including Maori and European history.

15. **New Zealand Rugby Museum (Palmerston North):**

Celebrates the history of rugby in New Zealand, featuring memorabilia and interactive exhibitions.

16. **Whakatane Museum (Whakatane):**

Exhibits about Whakatane's cultural and ecological history, focusing on the local Maori population.

17. **Aigantighe Art Gallery (Timaru):**

An art gallery presenting a varied collection of New Zealand and foreign art.

18. **Faraday Centre (Napier):**

A science and technology museum in Napier displaying old technology and interactive exhibits.

SHOPPING

TOP SHOPPING LOCATIONS:

1. Queen Street, Auckland:

A lively boulevard with a mix of high-end retailers, boutiques, and touristy shops. Look for Maori-inspired artwork, greenstone (pounamu) jewellery, and Kiwi-themed souvenirs.

2. Cuba Street, Wellington:

Known for its diverse boutiques, Cuba Street is a terrific place to get unique clothing, local art, and quirky souvenirs. The Wellington Underground Market on Cuba Street is also worth exploring.

3. High Street, Christchurch:

This region is home to boutique businesses and exciting shops. Find locally crafted goods, Maori artwork, and New Zealand fashion.

4. Ponsonby Road, Auckland:

Ponsonby is a popular suburb with chic boutiques, art galleries, and specialist stores. Look for fashionable clothing, handmade jewellery, and Kiwi skincare items.

5. Golden Centre Mall, Dunedin:

Dunedin's major shopping centre offers a mix of fashion, accessories, and local businesses. Look for Otago-themed gifts and Maori artwork.

6. The Arts Centre Market, Christchurch:

Held in the historic Arts Centre, this market showcases homemade products, local art, and unusual gifts. Ideal for one-of-a-kind presents.

7. Hannahs Lane, Palmerston North:

It is a beautiful alley with boutique boutiques and cafes. Look for locally created products, Maori artwork, and New Zealand-made clothes.

8. Sylvia Park, Auckland:

One of New Zealand's largest shopping malls, Sylvia Park includes many stores, significant merchants and boutique shops.

9. Wellington Night Market:

Held on Friday and Saturday nights, the market provides a variety of street cuisine, homemade crafts, and unusual souvenirs.

10. Duty-Free Shopping at Airports:

Auckland and Christchurch airports provide duty-free shopping with New Zealand products, including wines, chocolates, and skincare.

UNIQUE SOUVENIRS:

- Greenstone (Pounamu) Jewelry:

Carved from New Zealand jade, greenstone jewellery is a popular and meaningful souvenir. Look for necklaces, earrings, and bracelets.

- Maori Art and Carvings:

Authentic Maori carvings and artwork represent the rich cultural heritage of New Zealand. These make wonderfully unusual and significant souvenirs.

- Kiwi-Themed Gifts:

Kiwi birds are an emblem of New Zealand. Look for Kiwi-themed gifts such as cuddly toys, keychains, and artwork.

- Manuka Honey Products:

New Zealand is famous for its Manuka honey. Consider buying Manuka honey, skincare items, or honey-infused snacks as mementoes.

- Possum Merino Clothing:

Possum merino is a warm and luscious mixture. Look for clothing items like scarves, gloves, and sweaters from this distinctive material.

- Kiwiana Gifts:
- Kiwiana refers to products that are quintessentially New Zealand. This includes jandals (flip-flops), All Blacks souvenirs, and Buzzy Bee toys.

- Rimu Wood Products:

Rimu is a native New Zealand timber. Look for Rimu wood objects such as bowls, coasters, and artwork for a touch of local craftsmanship.

- Wine and Craft Beer:

New Zealand is famed for its wines and speciality breweries. Bring back a bottle of local wine or craft brews as a beautiful souvenir.

Chapter 6: Food and Drinks

LOCAL CUISINES

- **Fish and Chips:** It is a classic takeaway dish that is a mainstay of New Zealand cuisine. The dish consists of battered fish and deep-fried chips and is commonly served with tomato sauce and lemon wedges.

- **Hangi:** An ancient Maori way of cooking that involves slow-cooking meals underground. Meat, such as lamb or chicken, and vegetables are placed in a pit with heated rocks and covered with dirt, resulting in a smokey, savoury dish.

Where to Try: Look for cultural experiences or Maori cultural events that offer Hangi cuisine.

- **Pavlova:**

A renowned delicacy, Pavlova is a meringue-based dish with a crisp top and a soft marshmallow-like inside. It's often served with whipped cream and fresh fruits like kiwi and strawberries.

Where to Try: Various cafes and dessert locations across the country.

- **Kiwi Burger:**

The Kiwi Burger is a New Zealand variation on the basic hamburger. It commonly features a beef patty topped with beetroot, fried egg, lettuce, tomato, cheese, and sauces.

Where to Try: Local burger joints and cafes.

- **Pies:**

New Zealanders have a profound passion for savoury pies. These handheld pastries contain various ingredients, such as minced meat, sirloin, veggies, and rich sauce.

Where to Try: Bakeries and cafes throughout the country.

- **Whitebait Fritters:**

Whitebait are tiny, delicate fish, and Whitebait Fritters display them in a simple yet delectable way. The white bait is combined with eggs and lightly pan-fried.

Where to Try: Seafood eateries and beach regions.

- **Kumara (Sweet Potato):**

Kumara is a sweet potato variety commonly used in New Zealand cuisine. It can be roasted, mashed, or converted into Kumara Chips (fries).

Where to Try: Restaurants and traditional Kiwi BBQs.

- **Hokey Pokey Ice Cream:**

Hokey Pokey is a traditional New Zealand ice cream flavour containing vanilla ice cream with small, crispy toffee chunks.

It's a pleasant and famous treat.

Where to Try: Ice cream parlors and dessert shops.

- **Lamb:**

New Zealand is famed for its high-quality lamb. Whether roasted, grilled, or in a stew, Kiwi lamb is soft, tasty, and a mainstay in many households.

Where to Try: Restaurants and traditional Kiwi barbecues.

- **Green-Lipped Mussels:**

These giant mussels are unique to New Zealand and are commonly served steamed, grilled, or in seafood chowders. Where to Try: Seafood eateries and seaside locales.

- **Feijoa:**

Feijoa has a unique flavour profile that combines sweetness with a moderately acidic and tropical taste.

MODERN DISHES

- **Lamb Rack with Manuka Honey Glaze:**

A modern spin on classic New Zealand lamb sometimes served with a glaze created from locally obtained Manuka honey.

- **Crayfish (Lobster) Salad:**

Fresh crayfish served in a salad with colourful greens and a citrus-infused vinaigrette, showcasing New Zealand's seafood.

- **Venison Fillet with Red Wine Reduction:**

New Zealand's high-quality venison, commonly served as a fillet with a rich red wine reduction, accentuates the country's game meats.

- **Green-Lipped Mussel Risotto:**

Green-lipped mussels, peculiar to New Zealand, are combined into a creamy and savoury risotto.

- **Kiwi Burger with Beetroot:**

A modern take on the basic burger, the Kiwi Burger commonly features a beef patty topped with beetroot, fried egg, lettuce, tomato, cheese, and sauces.

- **Hokey Pokey Ice Cream:**

A popular New Zealand ice cream flavour is incorporating vanilla ice cream with little, crispy toffee bits known as "hokey pokey."

Kina (Sea Urchin) Sushi:

Modern seafood cuisine could include kina served as sushi, showcasing the rich marine life of New Zealand.

- **Manuka Honey and Walnut Panna Cotta:**

A trendy delicacy that mixes the sweetness of Manuka honey with the smoothness of panna cotta, topped with candied walnuts.

LOCAL DRINKS

- **Sauvignon Blanc:**

New Zealand is highly known for its Sauvignon Blanc wines. The Marlborough region, in particular, produces crisp and aromatic Sauvignon Blanc with unique tropical and citrus characteristics.

- **Pinot Noir:**

Central Otago and neighbouring locations are noted for producing superb Pinot Noir wines. These red wines are noted for their elegance, complexity, and rich cherry notes.

- **Manuka Honey Liqueur:**

This liqueur mixes the sweetness of Manuka honey, recognized for its health benefits, with a touch of alcohol. It's a unique and tasty drink.

- **Feijoa Cider:**

New Zealand's enthusiasm for feijoa extends to beverages, and feijoa cider is a refreshing and delicious alternative to classic apple cider.

- **L&P (Lemon & Paeroa):**

L&P is a popular New Zealand soft drink that originated in Paeroa. It combines lemon taste with mineral water, creating a distinctive and memorable Kiwi beverage.

- **Whittaker's Chocolate Milk:**

Produced by the well-known chocolate brand Whittaker's, this chocolate milk has earned a cult following. It's a rich and decadent delight for chocolate lovers.

- **RTDs (Ready-to-Drink):**

New Zealand produces a variety of ready-to-drink beverages, including pre-mixed cocktails and flavoured alcoholic drinks. They are convenient solutions for casual settings.

- **Hawke's Bay Chardonnay:**

Hawke's Bay is famed for its Chardonnay wines, which are frequently full-bodied with stone fruit, lemon, and oak aromas.

- **Craft Beers:**

The craft beer market in New Zealand has flourished, with various brewers making a wide range of innovations

- **Kokako Coffee:**

New Zealand takes its coffee seriously, and Kokako is a speciality coffee company noted for its high-quality, ethically sourced beans. Try a flat white or espresso for an authentic Kiwi coffee experience.

- **Pohutukawa Punch:**

Named after the famed Pohutukawa tree, this non-alcoholic punch blends fruit liquids and soda. It's a favourite choice for festive occasions and summer gatherings.

- **Tui Beer:**

Tui is a well-known beer brand in New Zealand, and their lager is a local favourite. The brand is also noted for its hilarious and unusual advertising.

- **Manuka Tea:**

Made from the leaves of the Manuka shrub, this herbal tea is considered to provide medicinal advantages. It has a mellow, earthy flavour and is generally loved for its relaxing effects.

- **Kiwifruit Liqueur:**

Kiwifruit, another classic New Zealand export, is made into a beautiful liqueur. Enjoy it as a shot or incorporate it into cocktails to taste Kiwi sweetness.

- **Tuatara Brewing Company Beers:**

Tuatara is a well-respected craft brewery in New Zealand, producing a variety of beers, including pale ales, IPAs, and stouts. Explore their broad assortment of flavours.

- **Riwaka Sour:**

Riwaka hops are famous for their unusual citrusy scent, and some breweries produce sour beers with these hops. The outcome is a pleasant and tart beverage.

- **Kawakawa Infused Gin:**

Building on the popularity of New Zealand gin, some distilleries infuse their gin with native Kawakawa leaves, imparting a characteristic herbal aroma to the spirit.

- **Moa Beer:**

Moa is a boutique brewery noted for its unique and high-quality beers. Explore their selection, which includes pale ales, lagers, and speciality brews.

- **Raspberry Lemonade:**

Locally manufactured raspberry lemonade is a delightful, non-alcoholic choice for hot summer days. Look for handcrafted versions in markets and cafes.

- **Totara Tonic:**

Totara is a native tree in New Zealand, and some companies create tonic water laced with Totara extracts. It's a new spin on a classic mixer.

- **Chocolate Velvet:**

This luxurious hot beverage combines hot chocolate with a shot of espresso, producing a decadent treat for chocolate and coffee lovers.

STREET FOOD

- **Hangi Pasty:**

A modern variation on the traditional Maori hangi, a hangi pasty consists of hangi-cooked meats and veggies enveloped in pastry, making it easy to consume on the go.

- **Hot Chips (French Fries) with Aioli:**

Hot chips are a frequent street food snack, often served with a side of aioli, a garlic-infused mayonnaise.

- **Puha and Paua Fritters:**

Puha is a typical Maori green vegetable, while paua is abalone. Cakes made with these ingredients can be found at various street food festivals.

- **Mussels with Garlic Butter Sauce:**

Street food events with a seafood concentration may serve mussels cooked in a delicious garlic butter sauce—a wonderful and aromatic treat.

- **Māori Fried Bread (Rewena Paraoa):**

Māori fried bread, or Rewena Paraoa, is a popular street dish with various toppings, such as butter or jam.

- **Southland Cheese Roll:**

A South Island delicacy, the Southland cheese roll has a mixture of grated cheese, onion soup mix, and evaporated milk folded in bread and cooked till golden.

- **Falafel Wrap:**

Vegetarian and vegan-friendly falafel wraps with chickpea patties, fresh vegetables, and savoury sauces are a great option.

- **Samosas:**

Triangular pastries packed with spiced veggies, meat, or a combination of both, samosas offer a delightful and portable snack.

- **Seafood Chowder in a Bread Bowl:**

Creamy seafood chowder served in a hollowed-out bread bowl is a substantial, comforting street food alternative.

Döner Kebab:

Inspired by Turkish cuisine, döner kebabs comprise thinly sliced, seasoned meat (typically lamb or chicken) served on flatbread with fresh veggies and sauces.

- **Banh Mi:**

A blend of French and Vietnamese flavours, banh mi, is a baguette stuffed with a variety of ingredients, such as grilled pork, pickled veggies, and herbs.

- **Caramel Slice:**

A popular sweet dessert, caramel slice consists of a biscuit foundation, caramel filling, and a chocolate covering. It's a sumptuous street food dessert.

- **Portobello Mushroom Burger:**

Catering to vegetarian inclinations, a Portobello mushroom burger is a tasty alternative, commonly grilled and served with various toppings.

- **Gourmet Sausages:**

Street food vendors specializing in gourmet sausages offer unique and high-quality sausage options, often served in a bun.

- **Ceviche Tostadas:**

Fresh and zesty, ceviche tostadas are comprised of marinated raw fish or seafood topped with salsa and served on a crispy tortilla.

- **Fried Pickles:**

Crispy and sour, fried pickles are a favourite snack. Pickles are coated in batter and fried till golden brown, offering a unique street food experience.

- **Sticky Date Pudding:**

A classic dessert, sticky date pudding is a thick, moist cake covered with a delectable caramel sauce—perfect for gratifying a sweet appetite.

- **Saffron-Infused Mussels:**

Mussels laced with saffron and grilled to perfection give a gourmet seafood experience that shows New Zealand's excellent shellfish.

- **Smoked Salmon Bagel:**

A popular street food breakfast or brunch choice, a smoked salmon bagel is commonly served with cream cheese, capers, and red onion.

LOCAL EATERIES

- **Fergburger, Queenstown:**

Dish: Classic Fish and Chips.

Renowned for its signature Kiwi experience, Fergburger gives you golden, crispy perfection with New Zealand's favourite fish and chips.

- **The Strawberry Patch, Matakana:**

Dish: Pavlova topped with fresh fruits.

The Strawberry Patch in Matakana makes Pavlova a national delicacy with finesse, creating a delightful symphony of flavours.

- **Te Puia, Rotorua:**

Dish: Hangi – Maori slow-cooked feast.

Imagine a real Maori culinary experience with Te Puia's traditional Hangi, a slow-cooked feast with meat and vegetables.

- **Flight Coffee Hangar, Wellington:**

Drink: Flat White.

Experience Kiwi coffee culture at its best with a finely brewed flat white at Flight Coffee Hangar in Wellington.

- **Jimmy's Pies, Roxburgh:**

Dish: Classic savory pies.

Jimmy's Pies in Roxburgh offers handheld pleasures, ranging from classic mince and cheese to innovative combinations, pleasing every pallet.

- **The Whitebait Stand, Haast:**

Dish: Whitebait Fritters.

Delve into subtle, marine aromas with The Whitebait Stand's delectable whitebait fritters.

- **Fleur's Place, Moeraki:**

Dish: Kaimoana (Seafood) specialities.

Fleur's Place in Moeraki celebrates seafood with a daily menu, depending on the catch, delivering an actual ocean-to-table experience.

- **Garage Project, Wellington:**

Drink: Assorted Craft Beers.

Explore creative and expertly brewed beers in the vibrant ambience of Garage Project, a significant name in New Zealand's craft beer market.

- **Federal Delicatessen, Auckland:**

Must-Try Dish: Pastrami Sandwich.

A flavour of New York in Auckland, Federal Delicatessen is famous for its piled pastrami sandwiches.

- **Ortega Fish Shack, Wellington:**

Must-Try Dish: Seafood Chowder.

With a focus on fresh seafood, Ortega Fish Shack's seafood chowder is a cosy bowl of maritime delight.

- **Penny Black Bar, Christchurch:**

Must-Try Drink: Kiwi Mule.

Penny Black Bar gives a kiwi spin to the classic Moscow Mule with the refreshing kiwi.

- **Pegasus Bay Winery, Waipara:**

Must-Try Dish: Peking duck.

Pair award-winning wines with savoury foods like Peking duck at Pegasus Bay Winery in Waipara.

- **Giapo, Auckland:**

Must-Try Dessert: Ice Cream Innovations.

Giapo in Auckland redefines ice cream, creating unique and artistic compositions that are as wonderful to the eyes as to the taste senses.

- **Cassels & Sons Brewing Co., Christchurch:**

Must-Try Drink: Milk Stout.

Known for its intimate ambience, Cassels & Sons Brewing Co. provides a rich and velvety milk stout that's a local favourite.

- **BurgerFuel, Various Locations:**

Must-Try Burger: The Bastard.

BurgerFuel is a Kiwi-born brand famed for its gourmet burgers, and The Bastard is a fan favourite with its unique blend of tastes.

- **Little Bird Organics, Auckland:**

Must-Try Dish: Raw Vegan Cheesecake.

Why Visit: Little Bird Organics is a paradise for plant-based fans, delivering scrumptious raw vegan sweets like their famed cheesecake.

- **Pomeroys Old Brewery Inn, Christchurch:**

Must-Try Dish: Lamb Shank Pie.

With a pleasant pub environment, Pomeroy's Old Brewery Inn is noted for its substantial Lamb Shank Pie, a Kiwi comfort food classic.

- **Punanga Nui Market, Rarotonga (Cook Islands, but accessible from New Zealand):**

Must-Try: Fresh Island Fruit Smoothies.

While not officially in New Zealand, the Punanga Nui Market in Rarotonga offers a flavour of the Pacific with its vivid fruit smoothies.

- **Cafe Gusto, Nelson:**

Must-Try Dish: Eggs Benedict with Salmon.

Cafe Gusto in Nelson is a local gem, and their Eggs Benedict with locally sourced salmon is a brunch delight.

- **The Oyster Inn, Waiheke Island:**

Must-Try Dish: Fresh Oysters.

Situated on Waiheke Island, The Oyster Inn is famed for its fresh oysters, combining a taste of the sea with a lovely island backdrop.

Chapter 7: Health and Safety

VACCINATIONS

- Ensure that your routine vaccines, such as DTaP (diphtheria, tetanus, and pertussis) and MMR (measles, mumps, and rubella), are current. These vaccines are required for overall health and fitness.

- Hepatitis A and B: If you plan to engage in outdoor activities, try local cuisine, or stay for an extended amount of time, consider getting vaccinated against hepatitis A and B.

- Typhoid: Vaccinating against typhoid is recommended, especially if you visit regions with poor sanitation or interact closely with locals.

- Influenza: Depending on the time of year, receiving the seasonal influenza vaccine is critical to protect yourself and others against respiratory illnesses.

- Meningococcal Disease: Stay current on any specific vaccine recommendations for meningococcal disease, as these may vary depending on your age and travel schedule, among other factors.

- Tuberculosis (TB): Although the risk of tuberculosis in New Zealand is low, it is vital to consult with a healthcare physician about your travel plans to determine whether a TB vaccination is required.
- COVID-19: Stay up to date on COVID-19 standards and vaccine requirements. Check that you conform with current travel restrictions and have the necessary documents and immunizations.

PREPARING FOR A HEALTHY JOURNEY:

1. Consult a Medical Professional: Schedule a pre-travel checkup with your doctor before vacation. Discuss your schedule, previous medical records, and any specific health conditions.

2. Medical Kit: Create a simple medical kit containing supplies, over-the-counter drugs, first aid kits, prescription drugs, and other items your doctor recommends.

3. Travel Insurance: Get comprehensive travel insurance that covers unexpected scenarios, emergency evacuation, and medical bills. Examine

the terms and conditions of your coverage to ensure that they meet your requirements.

4. Water and Food Safety: Reduce your risk of waterborne sickness by eating and drinking safely. Consume purified or bottled water, and select well-prepared food from reputable suppliers.

5. Mosquito Protection: Use insect repellent, wear long sleeves, and consider using pesticide-treated bed nets if your travels take you to places where mosquito-borne illness is possible.

6. Sun Protection: The sun can be powerful in New Zealand. Carry sunscreen with you and reapply it frequently to avoid sunburn. You should also put on eyewear and protective clothing.

Dealing with Emergencies

CONTACTS FOR EMERGENCY SERVICES:

- Police: Dial 111 for immediate police assistance in the event of an emergency or criminal activity.

- Medical Emergencies: Dial 111 and request an ambulance for emergency medical attention.

- HEALTHCARE FACILITIES: Research the locations of hospitals, clinics, and pharmacies in the areas you intend to visit. Always keep a list of these persons on hand.

- TRAVEL INSURANCE: Confirm that your policy covers unexpected circumstances, evacuation, and medical emergencies. Keep your insurance information, such as your policy number and emergency contact information, easily accessible.

- Always keep a fully charged cell phone and memorize the emergency numbers. Inform a trustworthy person of your travel plans and make frequent check-ins.

- Always have a fully equipped first aid kit, including bandages, antiseptic wipes, pain relievers, prescription medicines, and other essentials.

- Natural Disasters: Recognize your surroundings and potential natural disasters like earthquakes or floods. Follow local restrictions and evacuation procedures.

- LOST OR STOLEN ITEMS: Report any lost or stolen items, including passports and jewellery, to your embassy or consulate, as well as the local police. Copies of critical documents should be kept somewhere else.

- ACCIDENTS AND INJURIES: In case of an accident or injury, call 911 immediately. If someone is seriously injured, do not attempt to transfer them unless there is an imminent threat to their safety.

- Carry a detailed map or use reliable navigation software to help you navigate your way around new places. Inform someone of your desired route and expected arrival time.

- In an emergency, collaborate with local authorities and follow their instructions. New Zealand's emergency services are responsive and well-trained.

- **Weather conditions:** Pay attention to the weather, especially if you plan on doing something outside. Prepare for changing weather patterns and implement safety precautions.

- Be culturally sensitive when dealing with emergencies. Recognize and honour area traditions and engage efficiently with people and emergency personnel.

- **Assistance with consular work:** Foreign tourists should contact their embassy or consulate in a significant emergency. They can provide guidance and assistance.

- RELAX:.Remaining calm is critical in any emergency. Evaluate the situation, prioritize safety, and follow established protocols.

CONCLUSION

As we reach the final pages of the "New Zealand Travel Guide 2024," it's time to distil the essence of our adventure into practical insights.

This book has been designed to simplify the intricacies of trip preparation and cultural exploration, ensuring that your adventure in Aotearoa is engaging and readily accessible.

Key Takeaways:

- **Discovering Aotearoa's Story:**

Key Insight: Understanding the history, culture, and geography of New Zealand is like reading the plot of a riveting novel.

Practical Takeaway: Embrace the historical roots, immerse into the local culture, and enjoy the distinct geography to enrich your trip experience.

- **Planning Your Ideal Journey:**

Key Insight: Strategic preparation is the compass that directs your perfect vacation.

Practical Takeaway: Utilize financial advice, determine the optimal time to visit, and collect necessary paperwork to streamline your vacation.

- **Navigating Major Cities:**

Key Insight: Each city is a chapter in the voyage, presenting a blend of natural beauties and cultural riches.

Practical Takeaway: Prioritize must-visit places, employ numerous transit alternatives, and immerse yourself in the local ambience.

- **Locating Ideal Accommodations:**

Key Insight: Accommodations are not merely places to sleep but crucial to the complete experience.

Practical Takeaway: Choose accommodations that fit your preferences, from hotels to hostels, enriching your experience.

- **Exploring New Zealand's Wonders:**

Key Insight: Sightseeing goes beyond ticking off attractions; it's about making enduring experiences.

Practical Takeaway: Immerse yourself in natural wonders, museums, and local markets, letting the experiences mould your adventure.

- **Savoring Local Cuisine:**

Key Insight: Food is a cultural journey on its own, expressing the heart of a destination.

Practical Takeaway: Try native cuisines, discover modern recipes, and appreciate street snacks for an actual Aotearoa experience.

- **Prioritizing Health and Safety:**

Key Insight: A safe journey is joyful.

Practical Takeaway: Stay knowledgeable about vaccinations, be prepared for emergencies, and prioritize your well-being.

Your Adventure Continues

This guide is your roadmap, but the experience doesn't end on these pages—it's just beginning. Each takeaway is a practical step, ensuring your journey is seamless, fun, and full of cherished memories.

Remember, simplicity is the key to a stress-free experience. Embrace the voyage, take in the vistas, savour the flavours, and cherish every minute.

Aotearoa welcomes your exploration, and with these practical takeaways, your experience is guaranteed to be memorable and effortlessly delightful.